Nostradamus

Nostradamus

Prophecies for the Millennium

BILL ANDERTON

Page 1: An early alchemist in his laboratory attempts to make philosopher's stone.
Pages 2 and 3: Details from portraits of Michel de Nostredame – Nostradamus.

This is a Parragon Book

© Parragon 1998

Parragon
13 Whiteladies Road
Clifton, Bristol BS8 1PB
United Kingdom

Designed, produced and packaged by
Stonecastle Graphics Ltd
Old Chapel Studio, Plain Road, Marden, Tonbridge,
Kent TN12 9LS, United Kingdom

Edited by Philip de Ste. Croix

ISBN 0 75252 545 X

Printed in Italy

Contents

Prophecy – Looking into the Future

Nostradamus is perhaps the best-known prophet of modern times, 'prophet' in the sense of his famous ability to predict the future. His methods for divining the future belong to a strange and mysterious world, a world that is far distant from our own. It is into this world that we are to delve to find out how Nostradamus made his predictions and to find out what they were.

In a perfect world, science and technology take the guesswork out of prediction – if something operates according to certain laws, then we only need to discover and apply these laws for us to predict what will happen in the future. This may well be the case where the laws of physics unequivocally apply but everyday life is

Below: Michel Nostradamus – physician, astrologer, alchemist and one of the best-known prophets of all times.

clearly not so simple as this. Take, for example, our inability to predict with confidence the weather a few days hence. We may know the prevailing climate patterns and can make sensible predictions based on them, but the future often brings the unexpected, those things which take us by surprise.

If predicting the weather is so difficult, how much more so is the art of predicting human destiny by scientific means. Clearly another approach is required, one which calls upon the deepest resources of the human mind. This is the strange world into which Nostradamus delved to bring forth his predictions. It is this world which we too will explore; uncovering the history of Nostradamus's own life and times where we will discover the seeds of our own destinies which lead us inexorably into the next millennium.

We will begin by examining the whole field of prophecy and methods of looking into the future, and follow this with a description of the life and times of Nostradamus. Then we will consider one of the main tools which Nostradamus used in his work, namely astrology, and also his psychic gifts. Next we will examine the prophecies of Nostradamus, or at least the ones which are relevant to our own times and our future. Finally, we will look specifically at Nostradamus's role and influence in predicting the events which will take us up to the year 2000 and so beyond into the next millennium.

Divine Inspiration

Left: Nostradamus believed that his prophecies were the result of some form of divine or spiritual revelation. His unorthodox views brought him into conflict with the Church authorities.

Prophecy means to 'speak by divine inspiration'; a prophet is someone who speaks about revelations received from a divine source. Nostradamus was certainly a prophet.

We often term the means and techniques for looking into the future as 'divining' or 'divination'. There are significant differences between prophecy and divination. Most notably prophets do not *choose* to receive revelations about the future and often resist this role. They feel that they have been selected as a vessel or transmitter for their prophecies, whereas divination is undertaken as a matter of choice. Also, divination is usually conducted in response to a particular question, while prophecy happens spontaneously. Prophets are often unaware of the significance of their messages.

Perhaps a reason why Nostradamus has proved to be so influential and why his name is known by so many people is that he was both prophet and diviner. He believed he was acting as a channel for some form of divine or spiritual revelation and was quite aware of what he was doing and what he was receiving. Also, he was well practised in the art of divination and put his knowledge to good use. He was able through his art to make contact with – as he experienced it – a divine spirit who would provide him with his prophecies.

Although there are differences between prophecy and divination, Nostradamus proves them to be compatible. Both involve tapping into the unconscious mind in a state of relaxed awareness, both diviner and prophet opening themselves up to be a channel for whatever may or may not pass through them. Great prophets of the past have achieved renown usually for the accuracy of their prophecies, but occasionally because of the opposite! Some, like Nostradamus, have made prophecies which are relevant to the coming years, and all seem to agree that we are in for a time of change and upheaval.

The Millennium Approaches

Opposite: Sixteenth century alchemists were the medieval forerunners of modern chemistry and were often engaged in the challenge of creating gold and silver from base metals. Nostradamus was an accomplished alchemist and used its arcane symbols in his predictions.

Below: Nostradamus was a skilled astrologer and often used astrological references in his text. This shows a zodiac drawn for an Indian prince's horoscope.

The end of a century is always marked by predictions of doom and disaster, and even more so when we come to the conclusion of a millennium. Ours is an age of great change and uncertainty. The rapid pace of technological change, threats to the environment, the shifting political scene in east and west alike, economic uncertainty, all these elements add to a feeling of unease about the future.

Perhaps predictions of future disasters are justified, perhaps not; only time will tell for most people. We, however, are in a unique position to consider the art of Nostradamus and its relevance and accuracy, as we are the people who will live through the years leading to and beyond the millennium.

This book contains extracts from the writings of Nostradamus which are of particularly significant interest to us, especially relevant in many cases to life in this century and beyond it into the future. You will find that the extracts are accompanied by interpretations to help unravel the peculiar language that Nostradamus employed.

His text used a mixture of French and Latin, dialects, alchemical and astrological references, and it was often couched in symbolism and then, to make matters even more difficult, jumbled up. He used other literary devices, such as anagrams, and even altered letters in some of his words. We will examine the reason for this in the next chapter, but the end result is that interpreting Nostradamus is far from straightforward. The commentaries that are included translate Nostradamus into a much more straightforward language.

A criticism of Nostradamus is that his prophecies are not specific and so are open to different interpretations. In some cases this is true, to the extent that any interpretation can be made of the prophecy and it becomes impossible to determine whether or not it can truly claim to have revealed anything at all. There is an important point to be made here, namely that Nostradamus often used the language of symbols.

This means that his words incorporate two distinct levels of meaning. The first is an underlying truth which makes them significant for everyone, the 'archetypal' aspect. The second is that they also carry personal truths, so that we can read into them our own interpretations. The mark of a great work of prophecy is that it is both universally significant and relevant on a personal level too. This is the secret power that lies behind the prophecies of Nostradamus.

His writing will be relevant to everyone, no matter when or where they live. We find in Nostradamus great predictions for our future – he is helping us to see them, in just the same way that he helps anyone to see the future who cares to look into his works.

Interpreting the Prophecies

Right: It is possible to consider Nostradamus's predictions in a similar way to that in which a Tarot card reading is performed. The chosen cards may be interpreted in the context of the individual's own circumstances, just as Nostradamus's verses may reveal different things to different people.

Below: Nostradamus would have been familiar with planetary configurations, such as shown in this beautifully-illustrated astrological chart.

Interpreting Nostradamus is rather like interpreting a Tarot card reading. The cards are represented by his verses. We may choose which 'cards' to consider, and when we do, we perform a reading by interpreting them in the context of our own circumstances. This means that the same verses, the same prophecies, can reveal different things to different people, it all depends on who looks into them and what they are trying to see.

So, this book contains the prophecies of Nostradamus, but because the way he wrote them and the methods which he employed influence the way in which they should be interpreted, we will also briefly consider the life and times of Nostradamus, together with a more detailed examination of his divination methods.

To avoid persecution, Nostradamus deliberately jumbled the sequence and obscured the clarity of his prophecies. They were received in the form of images which he converted and wrote in 'quatrains', or four-line verses. The quatrains were published in Nostradamus's *Centuries*. This first appeared in 1555, so you can see how long his works have been available to the world. There seems to be no lessening of interest in him today. Quite the contrary.

Some interpreters suggest that Nostradamus has predicted a series of cataclysmic events which would occur in the time approaching the millennium year of 2000. Commentators suggest that the year 2002 will see dreadful wars, while the world itself, according to Nostradamus, will come to an end in the year 3797. Astrologers confirm that planetary configurations over the coming years support Nostradamus's notions of natural and man-made disasters. We will examine both Nostradamus's psychic gifts and his knowledge of astrology, and the related subject of alchemy.

It is interesting to compare Nostradamus with a modern day psychic and seer who also made influential prophecies about the end of this century. This was Edgar Cayce who was born in Kentucky, USA, in 1877, and died in 1945. Like Nostradamus, he became renowned for providing expert predictions derived from psychic trance sessions on a wide variety of subjects, present and future.

His belief was that there exists a form of universal mind which it is possible for the psychic to contact. This universal consciousness contains everything that comes to pass. It contains all knowledge. He called it the Akashic Record.

Cayce's predictions were consistently gloomy. He predicted a series of cataclysmic events happening over a 60-year span, leading up to the year 2000. At the conclusion of this book we will look specifically at the prophecies made by Nostradamus for the end of the millennium and will compare some of them with those made by the modern prophet, Edgar Cayce.

Now we shall delve into the strange world of Nostradamus. Who was he? What did he do and how did he do it? What were his predictions and what do they mean? All will now be revealed.

The Life and Times of Nostradamus

Born in St Rémy-de-Provence, France, on 14 December 1503, according to the Julian calendar, Michel de Nostredame came from humble Jewish-French stock. He was brought up in the Roman Catholic faith, to which his family had converted from their ancestral Jewish religion out of understandable concern for their own survival amid an age of growing religious bigotry.

Opposite: An impressive picture of Nostradamus, 1503-66, after a painting by his son and translator, César.

In later life, Nostradamus's secretary and disciple, Jean-Aymes de Chavigny turned biographer to write *La Vie et le Testament de Michel Nostradamus*. In it, Chavigny made the fascinating assertion that the young Michel maintained that the earth was a sphere which moved yearly round the sun, as did the various planets. If this is true, it could be the first, scarcely noticed, example of his prophetic talent. At the time, learned opinion was unanimous in believing that a flat earth was at the centre of the universe.

Below: The humble birthplace of Nostradamus in St Rémy-de-Provence, France.

Nostradamus the Healer

The young Nostradamus, already well educated by his learned grandfather, quickly became dissatisfied with the ignorance and dogma of his professors. With medical science still virtually in the dark ages, Michel's observations about cleanliness and the potential hazards of bleeding patients fell on deaf ears.

Eventually he developed his own methods of healing, taking to the road to follow the course of the bubonic plague. Instead of bleeding, he prescribed fresh, unpolluted water and clean air, and he administered herbal cures. In Narbonne, Carcassonne, in Toulouse and Bordeaux, his healing skills saved thousands from certain death.

It may have been through his visions of the future that Nostradamus understood about the importance of sanitation and the existence of germs. The work of Louis Pasteur, the great 19th-century medical pioneer of microbiology and vaccination is anticipated in Nostradamus's writings four centuries before his birth.

The picture we should paint of Nostradamus is not of a crazy psychic astrologer, suffering from delusions of grandeur with regard to his prophetic powers, but rather one of a highly educated man, a scholar and medical practitioner who made concrete and practical contributions to his society as a result of his learning, intelligence and insight.

Nostradamus studied at Avignon and at Montpellier University, taking up medicine at the latter institute as his main subject. Graduating in 1525, he left academia to pursue a career as a wandering physician. The plague was rife at the time and Nostradamus soon gained considerable renown for his unorthodox methods of treating it.

The Great Plague Strikes

Right: As a young doctor, Nostradamus developed his own ideas about treating victims of the bubonic plague. Insisting on the need for fresh air and clean water, he worked almost alone to assist the plague-stricken town of Aix-en Provence.

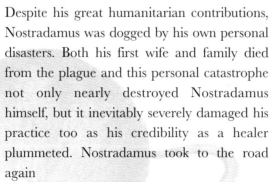

Despite his great humanitarian contributions, Nostradamus was dogged by his own personal disasters. Both his first wife and family died from the plague and this personal catastrophe not only nearly destroyed Nostradamus himself, but it inevitably severely damaged his practice too as his credibility as a healer plummeted. Nostradamus took to the road again

Most of his life at this time is unknown to us, but by 1544 the wanderer had returned, this time to Marseilles, where that winter's unusually severe floods, flushing out the rodents from their nests, brought renewed plague in their wake, and consequently more work for Nostradamus. The stricken town of Aix-en-Provence appealed to him for help and Nostradamus willingly responded, insisting particularly on fresh air and clean water for his patients. Working almost entirely alone, he became the acknowledged hero of the hour.

Nostradamus was indisputably much more than a prophet and successful clairvoyant. A famous doctor who had cured whole cities of the plague, he was also a gourmet and creator of fruit preservatives.

Occult Learning

A master astrologer, Nostradamus was avidly sought out by Europe's wealthy and noble citizens to draw up their horoscopes, and by their wives for his advice on cosmetics. He was also a noted translator of classics into French and wrote a comprehensive book called *Trakte des Fardemens* on the doctors and pharmacists he met on his travels in southern Europe. When travelling, he often stayed with physicians and apothecaries whom he respected, many of them also from ex-Jewish families, by day working with them to cure the sick, by night studying the occult under their guidance. These men participated in an underground network of alchemists and Kabbalists (those who studied the esoteric Jewish doctrine of the Kabbalah or 'Tree of Life'). They sought for answers to mysteries beyond the certainties preached by mainstream Christianity.

The events which led to the awakening of his prophetic powers centred around his being called by the Inquisition to defend himself on a charge of heresy. Nostradamus escaped under cover of darkness to wander around Europe on a journey of self-discovery, avoiding the Church Inquisitors and trying to piece together the fragments of his ruined life.

Nostradamus then married for a second time, this time to a rich widow by the name of Anne Ponsart Gemelle. Their house in Salon, which still stands to this day, has been renovated in his honour. At this time he largely abandoned medicine in favour of writing. Having converted the top floor of his house into a study, he committed himself to a much more all-embracing work: a vast collection of general prophecies. Little did he know how infamous these would become.

Below: Like many alchemists and Kabbalists in the sixteenth century, Nostradamus sought answers to the mysteries that were outside the teaching of the Christian church. He worked as a healer and physician by day, but studied the occult at night until he finally discovered his prophetic powers.

The Gift

Several famous anecdotes about the seer help to explain the reputation as a prophet that Nostradamus enjoyed during his lifetime. While travelling through Italy, he is said to have bowed before a passing young Franciscan monk, addressing him as 'Your Holiness'. The astounded onlookers could not understand this strange behaviour, but years later that Franciscan monk, the former swineherd Felice Peretti, became Cardinal Peretti and in 1585 he was elected by the College of Cardinals to become Pope Sixtus V. This occurred years after Nostradamus's death.

Another famous legend concerns the tale of the black pig and the white pig. While walking in the courtyard of the chateau of a certain Monsieur de Florenville, Nostradamus came upon two suckling pigs, a black one and a white one. He was asked by Monsieur de Florenville what would become of the two pigs. Nostradamus replied with certainty, 'We will eat the black one, and the wolf will eat the white one.'

To prove Nostradamus wrong and to discredit him, the lord ordered the chef to roast the white one on the spit and to serve it for their dinner. At dinner, Florenville again asked Nostradamus about the fate of the white and black pigs and Nostradamus maintained that what he had said earlier was true.

The chef was called in to refute Nostradamus's statement. All were astounded when the chef admitted that a tame wolf cub had nibbled at the white pig while it was roasting on the spit, and that he had served them the black one instead.

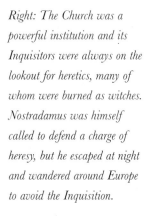

Right: The Church was a powerful institution and its Inquisitors were always on the lookout for heretics, many of whom were burned as witches. Nostradamus was himself called to defend a charge of heresy, but he escaped at night and wandered around Europe to avoid the Inquisition.

The Centuries Are Born

Left: Many great seers have experienced occult visions. Rembrandt's etching shows Dr. Johann Faust watching a magic disc appear in his study.

Above: The Column of Heresy, an engraving from an anti-Lutheran pamphlet dated 1526.

It was to his secretary, Chavigny, that Nostradamus first revealed his idea for a book of prophecy that would predict the future of mankind until the end of time. The book, to be called *The Centuries*, was to be set in ten volumes, each containing 100 quatrains (four-line verses). The completed text offers 1,000 predictions.

Work on *The Centuries* began on the night of Good Friday, 1554 and Chavigny records how, after each night's work, his master descended from the study with eyes and voice still glowing from a prophetic trance. *The Centuries* were first published in 1555. They were received enthusiastically by the upper classes and the nobility, a readership already well established by the almanacs – Nostradamus had produced a yearly *Almanac* from 1550 onwards.

Not all reaction to *The Centuries* was so favourable, however. The quatrains, written in a medley of French, Provencal, Greek, Latin and Italian, contained riddles and epigrams of bewildering complexity. To ignorant peasants, Nostradamus was a creature of the devil, his dark, cryptic verses hellish babble. From philosophers he drew both praise and curses, and poets were perplexed by the meaning of his verses.

Nostradamus's Night-Time Vigils

Below: This painting indicates the symbolism associated with alchemy. Nostradamus must have appeared to be a very mystical figure as he induced in himself semi-magical trances to invoke the divine inspiration that guided his prophecies.

Nostradamus's exact working methods are obscure, though they are sketched vaguely in the very first two quatrains. Most of his insights he seems to have gained by 'scrying' – in his case by contemplating the images that appeared in a water-filled vessel mounted on a brass tripod, either before or after using a wand to sprinkle his feet and the hem of his garment

with some of the contents of the vessel. He also appears to have induced in himself semi-magical trances in the course of which he heard mysterious voices. For months on end he seems to have spent much of each night in this way, since it was the best time to obtain the total silence and solitude he needed.

It is often stated that the reason Nostradamus made his writings obscure was to avoid persecution, either from the religious authorities who had caused him such problems in the past, or from particular powerful individuals whose fates were predicted in terms which were not exactly what they wished to hear. These are reasons which bear some credence. However, it is more than likely that the quatrains are obscure simply because this is the way that Nostradamus experienced them, or received them, in his trance-like state.

There is no doubt that Nostradamus would tinker with the prophecies, but they would have been received by him in no particular order, and would have been obscured quite simply because of the symbolic picture forms in which they came to him – rather like dreams, they are messages from a world which does not follow our rules which are bound by time and space.

The great project, however, was never to be fully completed. When first published in 1555, it consisted of only the first three *Centuries*, plus part of the fourth. Even the 1568 edition lacked over 50 of the seventh *Century's* intended quatrains – though it did contain the prefatory letter to Nostradamus's young son César and an odd quatrain in Latin doggerel at the end of *Century VI*. Also included was a bafflingly symbolic prose synopsis of his predictions in the form of a rambling screed entitled *Letter to Henri King of France the Second*. In addition, 141 Portents and 58 six-line verses were incorporated into various subsequent editions, as well as eight additional quatrains for *Century VIII* and 13 new ones apparently intended for two extra *Centuries* that were never completed.

Fame and Fortune

Completed or not, the effect of the whole compilation was both immediate and electric. At once Nostradamus was summoned to the royal court, where he was fêted and consulted by everyone, not least by Queen Catherine de Medici herself. He was required to draw up horoscopes for all the royal children – a difficult and delicate task in view of the ill-fortune that, unbeknown to the Queen, he had already predicted for almost all of them in his *Centuries*, albeit in his customary oblique form.

To add to his problems, word reached him that the Justices of Paris were starting to make serious enquiries about his alleged magical practices. Nostradamus returned home to Salon, where his newly-acquired fame easily kept at bay any darker suspicions that were circulating about him.

So impressed was the Queen that she even called on the seer at his home in Salon. It is described how Nostradamus used the occasion to identify among her retinue the relative nonentity who would become the future King Henri IV.

Nostradamus Predicts His Own Death

Nostradamus approached his own death surrounded by the same sort of controversy that was his hallmark both during his life and ever since. Clearly, he was not a man who would fade into insignificance and was prepared to stake his considerable reputation on a prediction of his own end.

With fame and riches came the pain of gout, arthritis and dropsy. Nostradamus died rich and famous. At the age of sixty-two, during the night of 1-2 July 1566, just as he had predicted to his local priest the evening before, and in exactly the manner that he had apparently already described. The final prophecy in Nostradamus's last Almanac foretells his own death:

Once back from embassy, once garnered in
The kingly gift, all's done: his spirit sped,
The dearest of his friends, his closest kin
Beside the bed and bench shall find him dead.

Below: Nostradamus accurately predicted the time and manner of his own death, which occurred during the night of 1-2 July 1566.

Psychic Visions

It is difficult to define exactly what psychic powers are, or what a psychic experience is, because the experience is a personal one, it is subjective – it cannot be measured in any objective way. The simplest way to describe it is as a sixth sense, a way of experiencing something other than through our five physical senses. The experience itself is nothing extraordinary; psychic sensations coming in the form of thoughts, feelings, images, sensations, even smells. But the interpretation of where these come from and what they mean is controversial.

Below: Nostradamus packed his study with books, many of which were concerned with forbidden subjects, such as demons and infernal spirits. This picture shows images from a 'Book of the Spirits'.

In the past psychic abilities were particularly associated with spiritualism and contacts made by the psychic with those who were deceased. The association still exists today and an interesting modern phenomenon is the work of Dolores Cannon, an author who claims to have been in contact with the spirit of Nostradamus who has communicated to her interpretations of his writings which are relevant for today. By psychic experience is meant inner knowledge and awareness that are communicated in a way other than through the physical senses. It is a sixth-sense experience.

Working on the basis that everything in our universe is connected – including our relationship with the future – and that this sixth sense is a reality, it follows that it is possible to use it to penetrate beyond the veil of everyday reality to see into the future.

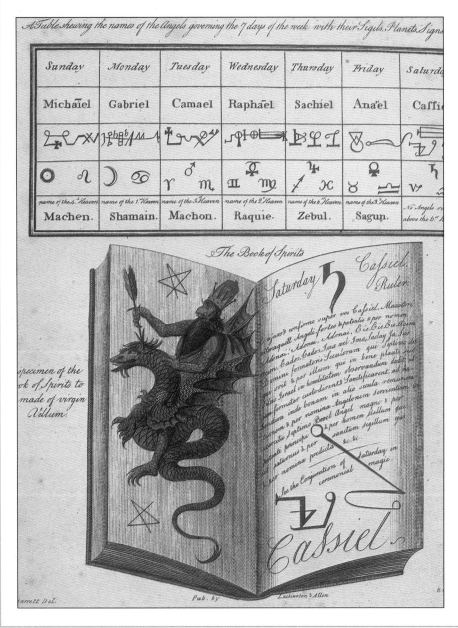

Nostradamus the Clairvoyant

A particular form of psychic experience is that of clairvoyance in which the clairvoyant's psychic sense communicates in terms of pictures. This is precisely the experience that came to Nostradamus during his night-time vigils.

There are other forms of psychic sense – clairaudience means receiving thoughts and words rather than images, for example.

Because the clairvoyant experience arrives in the form of images, the process – and its interpretation – has much in common with understanding precognition in dreams. Developing clairvoyance is a creative process involving the encouragement of one's imagination, rather like daydreaming but in a controlled and purposeful way. Nostradamus was an adept at this art.

Above: Demons riding to the Sabbath, from a medieval woodcut.

Inside Nostradamus's Study

The top floor of his house was converted into a study. It was packed with books. Some concerned medicine and astrology. The two went hand in hand in those days. But there were many more on darker subjects: forbidden works like *De Mysteriis Egptorum* ('Of the Mysteries of the Egyptians') by the Neo-Platonist Iamblichus, tomes of alchemy, and, most dangerous of all, Michael Psellus's fearsome *De Demonibus* ('On Demons') and that notorious grimoire *The Key of Solomon*, a guide to the evocation of infernal spirits.

There would also have been magical equipment. This would have consisted of a brass tripod, a small lamp or candle, the flame of which provided the room's only light, a wand, probably of laurel, and a bowl containing water. The atmosphere would have been pervaded by the smell of incense.

The Key of Solomon indicated elaborate preparations, but once complete its promise was 'Then will spirits appear and approach, from every side.' Nostradamus may not have gone so far as to invoke spirits. We do know, however, that he placed his laurel wand upon the tripod and wet his feet using the water in the bowl. Then, using the same water, he moistened the hem of his robe. These were

simple enough actions, but they reflected something deep, ancient and mysterious.

According to Nostradamus, as he completed a ritual a voice sounded which filled him with such terror that his arms trembled. Then, out of the darkness strode the splendid figure of a god, who took his seat upon the tripod stool.

Below: Nostradamus was interested in the mysteries of the ancient Egyptian civilization, and would, no doubt, have been familiar with the type of hieroglyphic writing that appears on this papyrus 'Book of the Dead'.

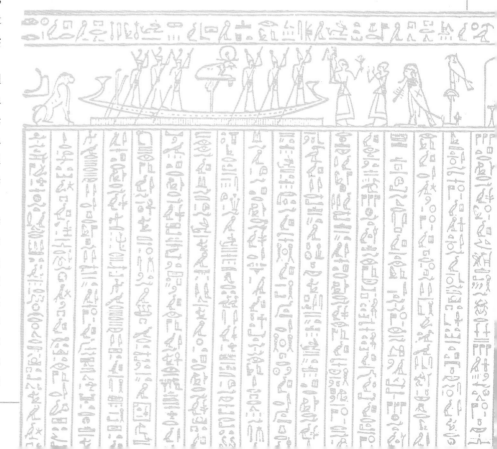

Magical Arts

Nostradamus used a variety of magical arts to induce ecstatic trances. Visions came to him through flame or water-gazing, sometimes both together.

The practice of water-gazing is similar to the use of a crystal ball and is called 'scrying'. This is best performed by candlelight in a darkened room, with the glass ball placed against a black background. If water is used, this should be in a black bowl, so that mental images are formed more easily. The idea is to 'see' images in the glass or the water. Imagine that you see things in them, just as when daydreaming or in guided fantasy, but your imaginations are projected into the crystal ball.

Nostradamus also followed the practice of Branchus, a Delphic prophetess of ancient Greece, which required him to sit, spine erect, on a brass tripod, the legs of which were angled at the same degree as the apex of Egyptian pyramids. The upright position, and possibly the use of nutmeg, which has a mild hallucinogenic effect when ingested in quantity, stimulated the mind. The angle at which the tripod legs were set was thought to create a force which would sharpen psychic powers.

Alternatively Nostradamus would stand or sit before a tripod that supported a brass bowl filled with steaming water and pungent oils. Between deep inhalations of perfumed vapour he would chant magical incantations:

I emptied my soul, brain and heart of all care and attained a state of tranquillity and stillness of mind which are prerequisites for predicting by means of the brass tripod.

The first stages of trance begin:

The prophetic heat approaches…like rays of the sun casting influences on bodies both elementary and non-elementary…

When the moment was auspicious, Nostradamus would dip a laurel branch into the steaming bowl and anoint his foot and hem. By so doing he released a rush of paranormal energy which propelled him into another dimension. In fire and water-gazing he then saw what he described as a 'clouded vision of great events'. Such visions were achieved by a union with what he called, 'the divine one'.

Carrying out the elaborate magical rituals apparently helped Nostradamus to overcome

Below: An illustration from Splendor Solis Salomon, *a manuscript, dated 1582, that expounds the magical arts of alchemy.*

Left: An alchemist at work in his 'laboratory'. The alchemist's business was as much to do with conjuring visions, drawing up astrological charts and creating mystical 'atmospheres' as it was to do with chemical experiments.

Below: During his trances, Nostradamus sat, spine erect, on a brass tripod which had its legs set at the same angle as the apex of the Egyptian pyramids.

his fear before surrendering to the full ecstatic trance, of which he said:

Although the everlasting God alone knows the eternity of light proceeding from himself, I say frankly to all to whom he wishes to reveal his immense magnitude – infinite and unknowable as it is – after long and meditative inspiration, that it is a hidden thing divinely manifested to the prophet by two means…One comes by infusion which clarifies the supernatural light in him who predicts by the stars, making possible divine revelation: the other comes by means of participation with the divine eternity; by which means the prophet can judge what is given to him from his own divine spirit through God the Creator and his natural intuition.

All Possible Futures

Below: The Mercurial demon of the alchemic philosophers. From Giovanni Battista Nazari's Della transmutatione metallica, *Brescia, 1589.*

Interpreters tend to regard Nostradamus's prognostications as predictions of the inevitable, but Nostradamus's own attitude to them was much less hidebound than this. In a strange way, he was more in tune with modern scientific thinking in that he believed in the existence of a multiplicity of possible futures.

This meant that a prediction would see the outcome of a current track into the future, but this direction could be changed, and therefore so could the future outcome, by our own will and actions.

So, although Nostradamus had great respect for the spirits with whom he communicated, he did not believe that their predictions were inevitable.

Today, scientists refer to the ability to foresee the future as 'precognition' and they have worked hard for decades in an attempt to establish its reality. Dr Helmut H.W. Schmidt, a German parapsychologist now working in Texas, developed fully automated ESP (extra-sensory perception) test machines, including radioactive random event generators. Routine use of computers to record results and hold data has become a further benefit. And the

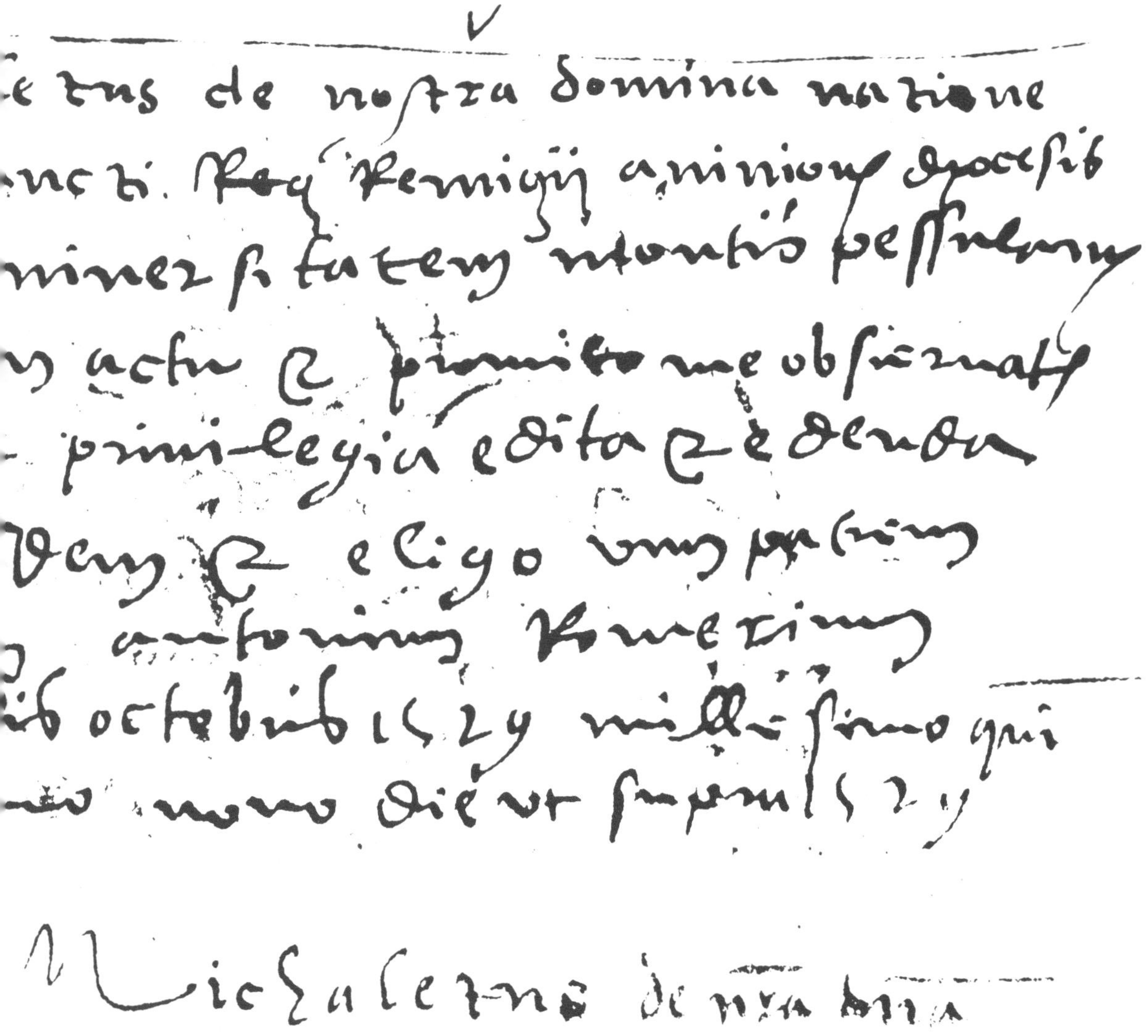

[Handwritten manuscript extract in Latin, showing Nostradamus's signature]

Left: An extract from the writings of Nostradamus, showing his signature. It is quite clear that Nostradamus was both learned and thoughtful. No one who studies his writings could dismiss them as the creations of a madman.

upshot has been that statistical evidence for the reality of precognition continues to emerge.

We have seen how Nostradamus predicted the circumstances of his own death, but his personal concerns did not end with his death. He seems to have been obsessed by the thought that people might walk across the grave where his body lay, for he left strict instructions that he should be interred upright in the wall of the local Church of the Cordeliers. In a rather more public document, he gave this macabre warning to anyone who might consider the desecration of his grave:

The man who opens the tomb when it is found
And does not close it at once
Will meet evil that no-one will be able to prove
It might have been better if he had been a Breton or
a Norman King!

Two subsequent events are worth relating. The first is that in the year 1700, the authorities of Salon decided to move the corpse and could not resist a quick look inside the coffin. Around the neck of the skeleton hung a medallion with the stark inscription '1700'.

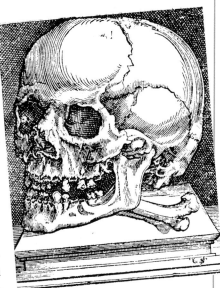

This was not all. In 1791 a contingent of national guards arrived from Marseilles, drunk and looking for trouble and they desecrated the grave. One of the guards even drank wine from the skull of Nostradamus on hearing that anyone who drank blood from it would achieve his psychic powers. Fortunately, there was no blood available. Unfortunately, later that day the guards were ambushed and the man who had drunk the wine was shot.

Nostradamus the Astrologer

Nostradamus was a practical and a learned man, a man well educated in the academic subjects of his day. These included the healing arts which were of special interest to him. And they also included astrology. His knowledge of this discipline, together with an understanding of the occult arts, alchemy and magic, were combined with his strong intuitive psychic powers to bring us his prophetic visions.

Below: Nostradamus was well versed in the art of 'mundane' astrology, which related to the prediction of world events, as well as that of 'electional' astrology, which was concerned with the timing and prediction of more specific events.

The Power of Astrology

It is worth spending some time considering the role of astrology in Nostradamus's predictions, for this gives an insight into the way that he was able to time his predictions, as well as describe the events that were to follow.

In Nostradamus's time, astrology was studied as a subject worthy of the greatest minds and it was generally accepted as being a valid and practical subject. However, the power of astrology was on the wane due to two factors. First, the Church's official doctrine limited what was and was not deemed suitable for study. This meant that astrology *per se* was not frowned on – but certain areas were, especially those to do with personal destiny.

Secondly, scientific method was becoming much more rigorous and was challenging the basis of subjects, like astrology, which had hitherto been accepted largely without question. Against the background of this prevailing atmosphere, Nostradamus undertook his studies and became proficient in the art of casting and interpreting horoscopes.

How Astrology Works

Astrology is based on the idea of cycles and patterns in life, which correspond with the cycles of the planets. Not only is it possible to analyse these cycles as they unfold in the past and present, study of them also gives a clue to the future too.

The astrologer's main tool is the horoscope. This is a map of the heavens drawn up for the time, place and date of birth. This can be established for any event – the birth of a person or an occurrence of historic importance. Conversely, as in Nostradamus's case, he could look at the patterns and relationships formed by the planets against the background of the zodiac and predict what events were likely to come about in the future. The birth chart shows the positions of all the planets, the Sun and the Moon, in the signs of the zodiac.

Astrology is based on a system of 'correspondences', which means that each planet, for example, corresponds with different ways of behaving, and different types of event. This is important in the context of Nostradamus's involvement with alchemy, a subject closely related to astrology and also involving the same system of correspondences.

Astrology appears to be complicated because of all the calculations that are necessary to formulate a horoscope. In fact the calculations are quite straightforward if time-consuming – Nostradamus did not have the luxury of a computer in his study!

Today we associate astrology with birth charts and personal horoscopes. This is called 'natal' astrology. Nostradamus's work revolved around different forms of astrology called 'mundane' astrology, which concerned the predicting of world events, and 'electional' astrology, which related to the timing and prediction of specific events. He was interested in both these areas. The church authorities found horary astrology (the branch of astrology concerned with personal problems)

to be unacceptable, but took a more lenient attitude to mundane astrology.

Even Catholics tended to believe in the influence of the stars, encouraged in this belief by the philosophy of Neoplatonism, but the basic problem for Christians was that it was impossible to believe that both God and the stars could rule human destiny, if God was to be credited as all-powerful.

A solution was suggested by Thomas Aquinas in the 13th century. Aquinas, who combined Christian theology with Aristotelian thought, drew a distinction between Natural astrology and Judicial astrology. The basic solution was that the body and the physical world were ruled by the stars, but the soul was ruled by God.

Above: In Nostradamus's time, astrology was studied by scholars and learned men, and was considered to be a practical subject that had great bearing on the events that occurred in everyday life.

Under the heading of Natural astrology were grouped mundane astrology (world and political cycles and events), medical and agricultural astrology. On the other hand, Judicial astrology dealt with personal destiny: natal astrology (the personal horoscope), horary astrology (answering immediate questions to personal problems, astrology 'of the hour'), and electional (predictive) astrology. The latter, which dealt with the timing of events in the future, was most frowned on by the Church. Papal Bulls were passed in 1586 and 1681 which banned the practice of these three areas of astrology, shortly after Nostradamus's death.

There is still some interest in mundane astrology today, the astrology of world and political events, but there are very few books available that explain it, simply because most modern astrologers are interested only in natal astrology, the interpretation of personal birth charts.

Alan Leo, who almost singlehandedly repopularized astrology at the beginning of this century, wrote in the introduction to his book on horary astrology:

Many who may be disposed to grant the influence of planetary action in relation to the newly-born, will nevertheless scarcely be prepared for the statement that it is just as possible to cast a horoscope for the birth of an idea as for the birth of a child, and to predict there from its nature, its progress, and its ultimate success or failure. Yet so it is; and while the degree of precision with which this can be done will of necessity vary with the skill of the individual exponent (as in all other arts or sciences), the mere fact that it can be done at all must make us ponder and reflect upon what many of us admit philosophically without at all realizing practically, namely that there is no such thing as chance. Divination by means of Horary Astrology then is a mere matter of fact, and is indeed largely practised, with surprising success, by many who are too ignorant or too superficial to probe the mysteries of Natal Astrology.

𝔑𝔬𝔰𝔱𝔯𝔞𝔡𝔞𝔪𝔲𝔰 𝔱𝔥𝔢 𝔄𝔩𝔠𝔥𝔢𝔪𝔦𝔰𝔱

Because Nostradamus was also an alchemist, we should consider exactly what that means to build a complete picture of how he made his predictions.

The beginnings of alchemy in the western world can be traced back to the time around the birth of Christ and it flourished in Greece during the second and third centuries AD. The Greeks did not experiment much with alchemy practically but tended rather to philosophize about it, developing theories about the processes of nature, how the world came into being, how it could be transformed, and so forth.

Another early influence on alchemy came from the civilization of Egypt; their occultists were not interested in theorizing, but they were interested in the magical effects of chemical experiments, which, not least, resulted in sophisticated embalming techniques, preserving the body for its after-death journey.

Greek philosophers theorized about all the basic concepts that are still fundamental to modern physics. Zeno discussed the problems of time, and Heraclitus that of energy. The concept of the atomic particle was elaborated and that of the four elements, ideas which persisted right up until the 17th century, even after Nostradamus's time. When the nature philosophies of the Greeks met the technological chemistry of the Egyptians, alchemy was born.

The most influential early text was the *Emerald Tablet of Hermes Trismegistus* (Trismegistus means thrice born), which became the alchemists' creed. The author lends his name to 'Hermetic' philosophy. The text of Hermes 'Thrice Born' is surrounded by legend but it probably originated in the early centuries of the Christian era. The text begins:

True it is, without falsehood, certain and most true. That which is above is like to that which is below, and that which is below is like to that which is above, to accomplish the miracles of the one thing.

And as all things were by the contemplation of the one, so all things arose from this one thing by a single act of adaptation.

The father thereof is the Sun, its mother the Moon…

Alchemy was, ostensibly, the search for a substance that would turn base metals into gold. This is the exoteric meaning of alchemy and the one commonly described by history books. Alchemical experimenters discovered the chemical properties of many substances in the course of their experiments and thus gave birth to chemistry. But if the search for a substance that would turn base metals into gold is a definition of the extraverted form of alchemy, then Nostradamus's search was concerned with a different form of alchemy. This was an inner quest, to get beyond the outer forms of the material world to the spiritual realities that lay beyond. Material gold in this context was a symbol of a much greater goal, a spiritual gold.

One of the main tenets of the Hermetic philosophy was that what was above (in the starry firmament) had a correspondence with what was below (in the world). Alchemists, like Paracelsus, believed that inside each person was an inner universe that corresponded with the outer universe. This meant that you only had to explore the correspondences of this inner universe to obtain knowledge about the outer events of the world, both now and in the future. This is precisely what Nostradamus did.

Alchemical texts are almost inaccessible when considered from the viewpoint of a modern sensibility, seeming to be illogical, inconsistent flights of fantasy. The texts and illustrations are rife with the sort of weird imagery that might be found not in the alchemists' chemical retorts, but in their

dreams. One of the key ideas of C.G. Jung's psychology is that the unconscious makes itself known to us through dreams and what he called 'active imagination', which is the conscious observation of inner images, rather like daydreaming, but in a more purposeful and deliberate manner.

These ideas are relevant to a study of Nostradamus because it is likely that he was projecting the contents of his unconscious, his 'inner universe', into his alchemical experiments. This is the basis of the method of scrying which was described earlier. The images which he observed would come from a deep unconscious level of his mind, the collective unconscious, giving us, in imaginative form, a picture of the human condition, past, present and future.

Below: Throughout history, mystics, prophets and alchemists have sought to contact the inner spiritual universe, often through dreams or visions which project the contents of the unconscious mind into the conscious world.

Astrology and Alchemy Work Together

Below: Alchemy and astrology are two sides of the same coin. Alchemy describes processes, while astrology describes the constituents of the alchemical experiment. The Sun is gold; the Moon, silver.

Alchemy and astrology are inseparable. Astrology describes the constituent parts of the experiment – the inner planets and what they represent. Alchemy describes the processes that take place in the alchemist's inner universe.

The chemical ingredients of an alchemical experiment included mercury, copper, iron, tin and lead, their combination leading to the production of silver, then, finally, gold. In the system of correspondences, each of the seven metals corresponded with one of the planets, which included the Moon and the Sun. More than this, it was said that each metal contained a portion of its corresponding planet and exhibited its particular qualities, expressing a link between a living personality (the alchemist), the planet and the metal.

Each corresponded with the other – as above, so below. The metal mercury corresponded with the planet Mercury; copper with Venus; iron with Mars; tin with Jupiter; lead with Saturn; silver with the Moon; gold with the Sun.

The external planet, or metal, Mercury has a correspondence with an inner, unconscious Mercury (as Nostradamus would have understood it), and it was the properties of this inner Mercury that were projected from the alchemist's unconscious into his or her experiment. Whereas today we can observe the outer universe through optical and radio telescopes, the alchemists and Nostradamus were observing their inner, unconscious universe by projecting it into their fantastic experiments, so filling them with symbols and mythological, irrational images, all of which appeared to have a life of their own.

One final observation here completes this description of how and what Nostradamus was experiencing. Many astrologers and alchemists believed that the planets – and in fact matter of any kind – were not inanimate, but in some way contained life, were inhabited by living spirits. This harks back to an ancient time when people believed that the planets were living gods who roamed the night skies.

It was, therefore, completely natural for Nostradamus to believe that, in summoning the images that dwelt in his inner universe, he was summoning living spirits to come to him and make their presence known in his alchemical retort.

Nostradamus the Astrologer

In his own words:

God's mysteries are incomprehensible and the power to influence events is bound up with the great expanse of natural knowledge, having its nearest most immediate origin in free will and describing future events which cannot be understood simply through being revealed. Neither can they be grasped through men's interpretations nor through another mode of cognisance or occult power under the firmament, neither in the present nor in the total eternity to come. But bringing about such an indivisible eternity through Herculean efforts, things are revealed by the planetary movements. I am not saying, my son – mark me well, here – that knowledge of such things cannot be implanted in your deficient mind, or that events in the distant future may not be within the understanding of any reasoning being. Nevertheless, if these things current or distant are brought to the awareness of this reasoning and intelligent being, they will be neither too obscure nor too clearly revealed. Perfect knowledge of such things cannot be acquired without divine inspiration, given that all prophetic inspiration derives its initial origin from God Almighty, than from chance and nature. Since all these portents are produced impartial, prophecy comes to pass partly as predicted. For understanding created by the intellect cannot be acquired by means of the occult, only by the aid of the zodiac, bringing forth that small flame by whose light part of the future may be discerned.

This quotation is taken from a preface to one of his books of prophecy, and is directed to his son, César Nostradamus. In it he strikes a note of caution by indicating that predicting the future is not a simple matter. It is made complicated by the fact that, although the information must be perfect as its original source is God, it is made imperfect by its transmission via the matter of the universe, and even more untrustworthy due to its interpretation by the imperfect human mind.

Above: A horoscope from the Zodiac tomb at Athribis, Egypt. Astrology was fundamental to the life and medical work of Nostradamus, and he used his knowledge of the planets and their movement through the zodiac to influence his healing.

In order to discover the truth, the interpreter has to work hard at improving himself so that his mind is worthy to receive the truth as given by God. It is possible to achieve the required perfection, but only through hard work and encountering many difficulties. There is help at hand, namely through the study of the planets and their movement through the zodiac. Astrology is one of the main tools to be used.

For Nostradamus, astrology was fundamental to his life and work; he attributed his healing power to a knowledge of the astrological composition of his medicines and his patients, and he was careful to administer cures at times when the aspects (relationships) of planets and constellations were favourable.

A century before Newton, Nostradamus's calculations show that he had an understanding of the laws of gravity and motion. Nostradamus plotted elliptical orbits for the planets in his horoscopes, preceding the establishment of Kepler's laws of planetory motion, as well as the astronomer Johannes Kepler himself who was not born until five years after the prophet's death.

Nostradamus's Horoscope

The birth-chart illustration is Nostradamus's own personal horoscope, cast for his birth on 14 December 1503 at approximately midday, Julian calendar. A modern astrologer would make some interesting interpretations. Nostradamus had a predominantly watery nature giving him an emotional disposition, one which related and responded to people and situations chiefly through the faculty of feeling. This endowed him with an emphasized sensitivity towards the intuitive faculty. Strongly sympathetic, even compassionate, he was often attracted to those less fortunate than himself, hoping to alleviate their suffering.

The most powerful part of Nostradamus's chart, however, revolves around the planets Jupiter, Saturn and Mars, conjunct in the Water sign of Cancer and opposite Neptune in Capricorn. This indicates an immensely powerful individual, his power stemming from his 'watery' intuitive faculties (Jupiter, Saturn and Mars) and finding outer expression through psychic, visionary Neptune.

This part of his chart alone sums up what we know to be true about Nostradamus. He was able to call on boundless energy (Jupiter) which stemmed from his unconscious, his inner universe. This 'inner' energy was converted into an outer form, making Nostradamus a tireless worker for the things in which he believed (Mars). And he was able to give concrete expression to his inner promptings. He was a practical man (Saturn), not an airy-fairy mystic.

The significant indicator in his chart is that these three planets, Jupiter, Saturn and Mars are all opposite Neptune. This planet rules the psychic faculties and in Nostradamus's chart this reveals a tremendous amount of power and significance. The opposition to the three planets tells us that in using this power he would be not only influential but would stir up a real storm, to the extent that his work would bring him great danger – and indeed this proved to be true. These configurations found in the chart of any lesser individual would suggest the road to madness, possibly through the misuse of drugs. Nostradamus was made of sterner stuff, and although his gifts caused him much suffering, he was able to ride and come through the storm to leave the world something very valuable.

Astrologers note also that Nostradamus's Moon was positioned in Scorpio, another indication of psychic powers and the ability to tap into the forces of the inner universe. The Sun conjunct his midheaven and also closely conjunct Mercury in Capricorn gave Nostradamus great intellectual powers which meant that he was taken seriously. Too often, psychic gifts are not accompanied by the necessary ability to argue their case in a convincing manner. Nostradamus was a man to be reckoned with.

Below: This horoscope is cast for Nostradamus's birth on 14 December 1503, according to the Julian calendar, at approximately midday.

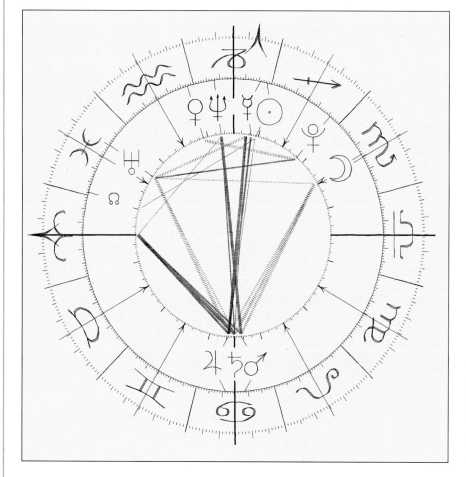

The Centuries

The scene has been set. Nostradamus was a man with a mission. He had studied hard, had applied his studies to the art of healing. He had developed his psychic gifts, learned astrology and alchemy and knew that inside himself was an amazing reservoir of predictive knowledge about the world in which he lived and the world to come. All this gave birth to *The Centuries*, the writings of Nostradamus in which he passed on his prophecies to the world.

In the next section are presented a selection of his 'quatrains', the four-line verses which have caused such a furore. These are the predictions of Nostradamus.

Left: Nostradamus brought all of his knowledge about the occult, astrology and alchemy to bear when he began his greatest project, the writing of his prophecies. He would have felt quite at home surrounded by the paraphernalia of the modern occult practitioner.

The Centuries of Nostradamus

Century I

Preparing For Visions To Come

Seated at night in my secret study,
Alone, reposing over the brass tripod,
A slender flame leaps out of the solitude,
Making me pronounce that which is not in vain.

(Verse 1)

Picture the scene: Nostradamus has retired to his secret room where he keeps his alchemical and astrological paraphernalia. He lights a flame under a tripod on which sits a flask containing a clear but steaming liquid. All else is dark as he stares into the flask and waits for the visions to arise

Nostradamus's Visions Are At Hand

With divining rod in hand, I wet the limb and foot,
Set in the middle of the branches.
Fearsome awe trembles my hand, I await,
Heavenly Splendor! The Divine Genius sitteth by.

(Verse 2)

And now Nostradamus senses that his waiting may soon be over. He begins to tremble with awe and expectation as he feels that the divine spirit which brings visions of the future to him is close by. To Nostradamus this process was a serious matter, not something to be taken lightly, and it involved nothing less than a spirit who would come to him, in time, when bidden by the magic which Nostradamus created in his 'secret study'.

Decline of the Roman Catholic Church

In the world shall be a Monarch,
Who will not leave peace, nor be long alive,
Then will be lost the Fishing Boat,
And shall be governed to its great detriment.

(Verse 4)

We come to the first of Nostradamus's significant predictions. Interpreters suggest that here is Pope John Paul II warning the world against materialism and war. When he is gone the Roman Catholic Church (Nostradamus's Fishing Boat) goes into decline and is lost. It is a warning about the blindness of capitalists to injustice within their economic system, injustices which stretch around the globe.

Left: 'The Papist Devil' – from a Reformation handbill, 15th century.

The Role of Emperor Haile Selassie in the Second World War

From the East of Africa shall come

the Lion-Heart,

To vex Venice and the heirs of Romulus,

Accompanied by the Libian Tribe,

Malta shall tremble and the neighboring islands

shall be empty.

(Verse 9)

The 'Lion-Heart' is said by commentators to refer to the Emperor Haile Selassie, who, during the Second World War, reconquered Ethopia in East Africa. The 'Heirs of Romulus' was the adopted title of the Italian Fascists, defeated by the Allies with the aid of an expedition 'From the East of Africa' sent by the Emperor Haile Selassie. The role played by the island of Malta as a key strategic point in conflicts involving the Mediterranean countries is clear.

The Russian Revolution

Being kept prisoners, by Princes and Lords,

The slavish people petition for songs and books,

For the future, idiots without heads,

Shall be received by divine prayers.

(Verse 14)

This is a reference to the revolutions in Russia during the 20th century, first the overthrow of the 'Princes and Lords' and the succession of the communist regime, followed by the more recent disintegration of the USSR in 1991, to be replaced by a commonwealth of independent states. Oppression results in control of knowledge (books) and even of artistic activities, such as musical composition and expression, both characteristic of the Russian communist government.

Above: A powerful image from the Russian Revolution – Orthodox monks lead a procession of striking workers, 5 February 1905.

Industrial Pollution

A deep white clay a rock supports,

Which shall break out of the deep like milk,

In vain people shall be troubled, not daring to touch it,

Being ignorant that in the bottom there is a milky clay.

(Verse 21)

The suggestion here is of the discovery and release of some new resource belonging to the earth, a substance that has perhaps radioactive properties which is mined and which troubled people dare not touch, fearing the consequences. Interpreters also translate this quatrain as predicting severe water pollution by industrial and chemical means, a problem which, once created, lies deep underground, carried there by waste disposal and in turn polluting water supplies which subsequently reappear above the ground. This may yet prove to be a major area of concern for the future. Remember too that Nostradamus's predictions are often of things unheard of in his own age, so interpretations of his verses must take into account the fact that he literally may not have known what he was talking about.

The Death of King Henri II

The young Lion shall overcome the old one

In martial field by a single duel,

In a golden cage he shall put out his eye,

Two wounds from one, then he shall die a cruel death.

(Verse 35)

This is one of the most renowned of Nostradamus's prophecies, namely the death of King Henri II of France. The Young Lion, a Scottish Knight, in a tournament with the Old Lion, Henri II, pierced his golden helmet with a splinter from his wooden lance, putting out his eye and penetrating the brain, causing the King's lingering 'cruel death' in 1559. Did Nostradamus know exactly what his quatrain was predicting, or did he puzzle over it? If the former, it was as well to couch such a prediction in somewhat ambiguous language to avoid the trouble for himself that such an overt prediction might have caused.

Below: The death of Henri II of France during a tournament for the wedding of Philip II of Spain. Nostradamus accurately predicted this fateful event.

A Witches' Assembly

The tenth of the Calends of April, Gothic account,

Raised up again by malicious persons,

The light put out, a diabolical assembly,

Seek for the bones of the lovers and Psellus.

(Verse 42)

Here Nostradamus sees an assembly of evil people, bent on the practice of the black magical arts. This assembly takes place in the dark on 23 April. The acts performed are according to a famed Byzantine writer on black magic, called Psellus. The 'diabolical assembly' may refer to those gathered, or more likely to spirits called up from the dead, from the past, to perform some diabolical task.

Above: 'The First Thanksgiving' of the Pilgrim Fathers in America.

The Origins of the USA

From the aquatic triplicity shall be born,

One who shall make Thursday his holiday,

His fame, praise, rule, and power shall grow,

By Land and Sea to become a tempest to the east.

(Verse 50)

The immediate response to the 'aquatic triplicity' is that this is an astrological reference to the Water signs of the zodiac, but in fact it refers to the oceans of the Atlantic, the Pacific and the Gulf of Mexico. Nostradamus is predicting the establishment of the United States of America, 200 years before it came into existence. The national holiday of Thanksgiving always takes place on a Thursday, while the USA has been, until recent years, the scourge of oriental lands, a 'tempest to the east'.

The Suffering of Native American Indians

Alas, how a great people shall be tormented

And the Holy Laws in total ruin,

By other laws, all Christianity troubled,

When new mines of gold and silver will be found.

(Verse 53)

Environmental Disasters

Alas, what a great loss shall learning suffer

Before the cycle of the moon is accomplished,

By fire, great flood, and ignorant sceptres,

More than can be made good again in a long age.

(Verse 62)

Commentators suggest that this verse predicts the discovery of rich mines in places such as Africa and Australia, where the indigenous people are oppressed, their spiritual laws destroyed and replaced by those of the invaders, who come in the name of Christendom, but who take what they desire by force. There is a suggestion that this also refers to the indigenous Native American Indian nations of North America, but it is a universal story of oppression and greed to be found in many places around the world since the rise of materialism and the decline of more ancient, spiritual ways of life. Nostradamus was quite clear about the ubiquity of this process.

This is a rather poetic description of forthcoming environmental disasters, resulting in a final cataclysmic day (the moon crashes into the earth on the completion of its cycle?). More prosaic is the suggestion that our current environmental problems, such as the loss of rain forests and the depletion of the ozone layer, are entirely man-made and occur simply through ignorance and greed. They are completely unnecessary and cannot be made good for the foreseeable future, 'in a long age'.

Above: Nostradamus predicted that the Native American Indian nations would be destroyed by the invaders who came in the name of Christendom.

Century II

The Death of Mussolini

The blue law shall do the white law

As much harm, as France has done it good,

Dead on the antenna, a great one hanged on a branch,

When a king taken by his own shall say, 'How much?'

(Verse 2)

The image of being hanged on a branch conjures up visions of crucifixion, the Tarot's Hanged Man, or even the sufferings of the mythological Norse god, Odin, who suffered this pain and in doing so achieved the gift of prophecy. Commentators suggest that this quatrain refers to the death of the Italian dictator Benito Mussolini at the end of the Second World War. On 28 April 1945, Mussolini and his mistress, Clara Petacci, were shot by partisans and their bodies were hanged upside down in Milan, Northern Italy. A plebiscite abolished the Italian monarchy in 1946, suggested in the stanza's last line.

The Creation of the Berlin Wall

Near the gates and within two cities,

Shall be two scourges, I never saw the like,

Famine, within plague, people thrust out by the sword,

Shall cry for help to the great God immortal.

(Verse 6)

Although this is a prediction of famine and plague, it is suggested that the 'two cities' in fact refer to one, namely Berlin, divided by its now defunct wall. The horrors of the Serbian conflicts in Bosnia are also suggested by this verse. Nostradamus can sometimes seem very vague when it comes to pinpointing the time and place to which he refers. Remember, however, that his prophecies were often accompanied by astrological predictive data.

Above: A west German policeman keeps guard at the Berlin Wall.

Left: Mussolini was hanged upside down after his death.

The Reign of Louis XVI

Nine years shall the lean one keep the kingdom in peace,

Then he will fall into such a bloody thirst,

That a great people shall die without faith or law,

He shall be killed by one much wilder than himself.

(Verse 9)

Less symbolic than most of the verses and more literal – and therefore easier to interpret – Nostradamus refers to the reign of King Louis XVI of France. His reign was marked by a period of peace at its beginning and ended with a revolution that was extreme both in the political sense, and also in the ferocity of its lawlessness and blood-letting. This reign culminated in the execution of the King in 1793 before the baying Parisian mobs.

Above: King Louis XVI of France. His reign ended with a revolution.
Above right: Nostradamus may have predicted the arrival of extra-terrestrials.

The Arrival of Extra-Terrestrials

The garrison of strangers shall betray the fort,

Under the game of hope of a higher union.

The garrison shall be deceived, and the fort taken quickly

Loire, Saône, Rhône, Garonne, outraged by death.

(Verse 25)

It has been claimed that the arrival of extra-terrestrials is not a thing of the future but that creatures from beyond our galaxy have been amongst us for hundreds, if not thousands, of years. Here, Nostradamus makes reference to 'strangers', which commentators have suggested is his way of indicating the presence of these extra-terrestrial visitors. These particular guests are, it is clear, certainly not to be trusted, for it is their intention to gain trust and then betray it, resulting in a defeat for the fort.

The French Revolution

A cock, dogs and cats shall be fed with blood,

And with the wound of the tyrant found dead,

In the bed of another with legs and arms broken,

Who could not die before by a cruel death.

(Verse 42)

Some of the images that Nostradamus conjures up are quite frankly repellent, especially as many contain references to painful death. This verse may refer to the death of a particular individual, namely Robespierre, the tyrant of the French Revolution who led the Reign of Terror. The French nation is referred to as the 'cock' and the rabble of Paris as 'dogs and cats'. Parisians were 'fed with blood' via the public executions at the guillotine, one of them being that of Robespierre. When seized he was seriously wounded, tied to a bed overnight and executed the next morning on the orders of the Revolutionary Tribunal.

The Great Fire of London

The blood of the just shall be dry in London,

Burnt by the fire of three times twenty and six,

The ancient dame shall fall from her high place,

Of the same sect many shall be killed.

(Verse 51)

Here is a remarkable vision that came to Nostradamus as he meditated in his secret study. The year is 'three times twenty and six', that is 1666, and the event is a great fire in London. Not only does Nostradamus predict this accurately, but he adds a rather incisive touch, telling that the 'ancient dame', the statue of the Virgin Mary on St Paul's steeple, falls from its place. Many would have prayed for her intercession in this disaster, but she was unable to prevent many deaths during this catastrophic event.

Below: Nostradamus accurately predicted the Great Fire of London in 1666.

Sino-Soviet Relations and the Great Wall

Before the battle, the great wall shall fall,

The great one to death, too sudden and bewailed,

The boat being imperfect the most part shall swim

Near the river the earth shall be dyed with blood.

(Verse 57)

This quatrain anticipates a Sino-Soviet war and the destruction of the Great Wall of China. The Yellow River intersects the Great Wall in Shansi Province where, on the outreaches of Peking, a great battle will be fought turning the Yellow River red with blood. The first line also foretells the destruction of the Berlin Wall, which was shortly followed by the 'great battle' – political rather than military in nature – in Russia.

Aircraft and Spacecraft

The noise of the unwanted bird having been heard,

Upon the canon of the highest storey,

The bushel of wheat shall rise so high,

That Man shall be a man-eater.

(Verse 75)

There is more than one reference in the writings of Nostradamus to 'birds' which have violent military applications. Here is one of them, with the unwanted noisy bird representing aircraft or spacecraft that allow man to destroy himself. Technology is a double-edged sword. On the one hand it gives us the ability to genetically engineer and create high-yielding food supplies. Feeding the world's population may no longer be a problem. On the other hand, the same ability to 'engineer' gives us the means to bomb humanity out of existence.

Right: Nostradamus referred to aircraft and spacecraft that could have violent military applications. He realized that the power of technology might be used either for mankind's good, or for utter destruction.

Britain's Recession

The great trade of the great Lion altered,

The most part turns into pristine ruin,

Shall become a prey to soldiers and reaped by wound

In Mount Jura, and Swabia great fogs.

(Verse 83)

The 'great Lion' is Great Britain, whose industrial trade and supremacy is predicted here to turn to 'ruin'. The reference is to the decline of the British Empire, the horrors suffered by British soldiers who fought in the First World War and the further suffering caused by later economic depressions, first in the 1930s and then, more recently, in the late 1980s and early 1990s. The suggestion is that Mount Jura (the Jura mountains stretch between France and Switzerland) and Swabia (Germany) have some direct bearing on these events.

The End of the Cold War

One day the two great masters shall be friends,

Their great powers shall be increased,

The new land shall be in a flourishing condition,

The number shall be told to the Bloody Person.

(Verse 89)

Rather like the scenario in George Orwell's novel *1984*, the great powers are constantly at odds with one another, and then forging new partnerships against a common enemy. Nostradamus foresees such a new partnership forged between West and East, between the United States and China, against the 'Bloody Person' who is told 'the number', or as we would say, their number is up! This quatrain is also taken as a prophecy of the ending of the Cold War between the United States and the Soviet Union.

Century III

European Theatre of Nuclear Conflict

The fugitives, fire of heaven on the pikes,

A fight near at hand, the ravens croaking,

They cry from the land, Help, O heavenly powers,

When near the walls shall be the fighting men.

(Verse 7)

This is a prediction for the late 20th century, and notwithstanding the demise of the Berlin Wall, it is taken by commentators to suggest that there is a theatre of nuclear conflict close to and around Berlin, with the raven, an emblem of Germany together with the black eagle, lending weight to this interpretation. Let us hope that in this instance, Nostradamus is proven to be wrong. Many of his interpreters lay emphasis on Nostradamus's predictions for a terrible war at the close of this millennium, and indeed Nostradamus himself placed great emphasis on this time as a turning point in human affairs.

Military Aircraft

Armies shall fight in the air a great while,

The tree shall fall in the middle of the city,

Vermin, scabs, sword, firebrand in the face,

When the Monarch of Venice shall fall.

(Verse 11)

Before Nostradamus's time, the great artist Leonardo da Vinci (1452-1519) had already presented the world with images that suggested the possibility of manned flight. Nostradamus would probably have been aware of his work. This quatrain takes the idea much further and suggests the application of aircraft for military purposes, envisioning the coming of great battles taking place above the ground. As we now know, it was in the 20th century that these particular predictions came to pass.

Below: A military aircraft, loaded with modern bombs and missiles.

Israel and the Six-Day War

Six days shall the assault be in front of the city,

A great and fierce battle shall be fought,

Three shall surrender it, and be pardoned,

The rest shall be put to fire and sword, cut and slashed.

(Verse 22)

This prediction is a reference to Israel's so-called Six Day War in which Israel's Arab enemies were comprehensively and swiftly defeated. In 1967, in response to Syrian border raids, Israel launched fierce air attacks against Syria, Jordan and Egypt. The Arab nations surrendered and released their captive prisoners of war. The Middle Eastern conflict has continued in one form or another to this day, a fragile peace being the current situation.

Above: Many of Nostradamus's predictions refer to the tyranny of Hitler.

The Birth of Hitler

Out of the deepest part of the west of Europe,

From poor people a young child shall be born,

Who with his tongue shall seduce many people,

His fame shall increase in the Eastern Kingdom.

(Verse 35)

This verse refers to the birth of Adolf Hitler, born of poor parents in Austria in 1889 and whose powers of oratory and knowledge of mass psychology are infamous. These gifts he used to the full with dire consequences for the western world. The verse refers to his fame in the east too, with an indication that his powers were admired even in Japan, a completely different culture to that of western Europe. Nostradamus made many predictions about the period of the two World Wars in this century and indeed much of his celebrity rests upon them.

France — From Monarchy to Republic

French Kingdom thou shalt be much changed,

The Empire is translated in another place,

Thou shalt be put to other manners and laws,

Rouen and Chartres shall do the worst they can to thee.

(Verse 49)

Another major area of concern for Nostradamus was the destiny of his own country, France. Hence, his prognostications are littered with references to the French Revolution. Here he predicts the transition from Monarchy to Republic, which turned out to be a very bloody process. Commentators also suggest that this passage is a reference to the formation in 1992 of the European Economic Community single market, within which France plays a key role. It is also a time of much change and economic upheaval in France's fortunes.

The Exile of Argentina's Juan Peron

One of the greatest shall run away into Spain,

That shall cause a wound to bleed long,

Leading armies over high mountains,

Destroying all, and afterwards shall reign.

(Verse 54)

Nostradamus's prophetic and psychic abilities allowed him to look further afield than the European theatre, and this quatrain invites us to consider the fate of Juan Peron, President of Argentina, who was sent into exile in 1955, fleeing to Spain. His country then suffered a period of chaos and misery, following which Peron was reinstated in 1973, taking control from the military junta which had made itself deeply unpopular in his absence.

Right: Juan Peron, President of Argentina, was sent into exile in 1955.
Opposite left: Nostradamus predicted war in the Gulf. Here, American troops march towards their transport plane after their arrival in Saudi Arabia at the start of the Gulf War.
Opposite right: Winston Churchill was defeated in the election of 1945.

War in the Gulf

The head of Persia shall fill great merchant ships,

A fleet of warships against the Mohammedan folk,

From Parthia and Media they shall come to

plunder the Cyclades,

A long rest shall be on the Ionic port.

(Verse 64)

Nostradamus is here predicting war in the Gulf and the associated oil crisis. He indicates that a great potentate sends a fleet of warships supported by a well-supplied group of commercial vessels to engage with a Moslem League. The result is stagnation of the trade in the Mediterranean and a subsequent short but bloody war. Persia (Iran) is the main antagonist, and the end result is that not only are the Ionic and Mediterranean ports at rest – and therefore their trade is at a standstill – but this is part of an embargo which continues to affect Iraq, long after the conclusion of the Gulf war.

Churchill is Defeated

The good old man shall be buried alive,

Near the great river by a false suspicion,

The new old one made noble by his riches,

The gold of his ransom shall be taken in the way.

(Verse 72)

The key phrase in this verse is 'buried alive'. Usually, Nostradamus's language is couched in enigmatic turns of phrase, but here is a modern expression used to suggest the occurrence of a landslide victory in a political, rather than a physical, battle. The verse refers to the heavy defeat of Winston Churchill after he had steered Great Britain to victory in the Second World War. The 'great river' is the River Thames, close to which these events were played out, resulting in Churchill's defeat in the election of 1945.

The Destruction of the Berlin Wall

The great city shall be made very desolate,

Not one of the inhabitants shall be left in it,

Wall, sex, church and virgin ravished,

By sword, fire, plague, cannon, people shall die.

(Verse 84)

This is a prediction that the Berlin wall will be destroyed. There is more than one suggestion in Nostradamus's works that Berlin will again become the centre of conflict and destruction. The removal of the wall in 1989 was seen almost universally as representing the end of an era of conflict and separation and the beginning of one of peace and reconciliation. Nostradamus had different ideas, according to his interpreters, who see this part of Europe as suffering further in the conflicts of the late 20th century. So, we have here another reference to the desolation which may yet be caused by nuclear conflict.

Nostradamus Vindicates Himself!

For five hundred years no account shall be made

Of him who was the ornament of his time.

Then of a sudden he shall give so great a light,

That for that age he shall make them to be most contented.

(Verse 94)

Nostradamus is complaining here that no one will take him seriously, but he knows that in the end his predictions will be vindicated. He even gives an exact date when the scales will fall from humanity's eyes, after 500 years in 2055. Although he may have felt unjustly ignored in his own time, it is not true to say that he did not at least achieve fame (and a degree of fortune) through his collection of predictions. His words are read by more and more people who are increasingly worried about the fate of our world and seek for some form of comfort in his predictions. There is little there, however, to ease our worries.

Above: Destruction of the Berlin wall in 1989.

Opposite: Edward, Prince of Wales, reigned briefly as Britain's king in 1936.

Century IV

The Common Market

The cross shall have peace, under an accomplished
divine word,
Spain and France shall be united together,
A great battle near at hand and the most sharp fight,
No heart so stout but shall tremble.

(Verse 5)

The suggestion is that Spain and France shall have military, political and eventually economic ties and indeed this has come about through the institutions of the European Community or Common Market. Nostradamus was making a prophecy here which perhaps few would have taken seriously – until it actually came to pass. Spain was a neutral country in the Second World War and then later in the century remained unaligned in the East-West power struggle.

Edward VIII's Short Reign

The young prince being falsely accused,
Shall put the camp in trouble and in quarrels.
The chief shall be murdered by the tumult,
The sceptre shall be appeased and later cure the king's evil.

(Verse 10)

Edward, Prince of Wales, enjoyed a short reign as King of Britain in 1936. He had courted controversy through accusations that he harboured Nazi sympathies. The reputation was an unfortunate one, but apparently had some substance – Edward established a special relationship with the German government during the 1930s and later he became an apologist for their aggressive behaviour. His intentions may have been honourable, hence the suggestion of false accusation, but the outcome was inevitable. He eventually abdicated the throne in 1936 in order to be free to marry the divorcee Wallis Simpson whom he loved.

The Kennedy Assassination and the Attempt on Reagan's Life

Two verses are relevant here:

News being brought of a great loss,
The report divulged, the camp shall be astonished,
Troops being united and revolted,
The falange shall forsake the great one.

(Verse 13)

This quatrain contains two messages. The first of these refers to the assassination of President Kennedy in 1963 and the ensuing plethora of reports and speculation as to who did what and why. Also predicted is the revolt against Franco and his dictatorship by the Spanish army and the political party known as the Falangists. The founder and chief Falangist spokesman, José António Primo de Rivera, was executed in November 1936.

The sudden death of the chief man,
Shall cause a change, and put another in the reign soon,
Late come to so high a degree in a low age,
So that by land and sea he must be feared.

(Verse 14)

This is a continuation of the preceding quatrain, referring to President Kennedy who became President at a 'low age' i.e., when young. Perhaps the fourth line refers to the Cuban missile crisis of 1962 when the USA and the Soviet Union stood on the brink of a nuclear war. The verse also fits the circumstances of the attempted assassination of President Reagan in 1981.

Science and Power

The most learned in the celestial sciences,
Shall be found fault with by ignorant princes,
Punished by a proclamation, chased away as wicked,
And put to death where they shall be found.

(Verse 18)

Although science has given mankind great benefits, it has also created the means for destruction. Science and scientists have become exceedingly powerful in the 20th century. Scientists often realize the potential destruction that their discoveries can bring about and warn about this. Here Nostradamus is imploring that these warnings should be heeded and taken seriously. For example, with regard to nuclear power there is an imperative need for international agreement and control.

Alchemy and the Philosopher's Stone

The Sun shall be hid and eclipsed by Mercury,

And shall not be set but for the second heaven,

Hermes shall be made a prey to Vulcan,

And after that the Sun shall be seen pure, shining

and yellow.

(Verse 29)

In this and several other related verses, Nostradamus makes allusions to his study of alchemy. The Sun is gold, both in material and spiritual form, and the planet or metal Mercury is the spirit Hermes, who created the philosopher's stone – the substance that will turn all metals into gold. Although Nostradamus is talking about the planets and the mythological smith of the gods, Vulcan, he is also telling us how to make the gold that we desire. The ability to turn one substance into another may have seemed unlikely until recently, but today it is possible through the process of nuclear fusion and fission.

Opposite top: Nostradamus predicted the assassination of President Kennedy.
Above left: The D-Day invasion of France by Allied Forces in 1944.
Left: Nostradamus was aware of the increasing power that scientists would wield in a nuclear age. Isaac Newton's discoveries seem gentle by comparison.

The D-Day Invasion of France

The plain about Bordeaux fruitful and spacious,

Shall produce so many hornets and so many grasshoppers,

That the light of the Sun shall be darkened,

They shall fly so low, a great plague shall come from them.

(Verse 48)

At the time of the D-Day invasion of France by Allied Forces in 1944 during the Second World War, the sky was darkened by the tremendous concentration of air power involved. Nostradamus equates aeroplanes with hornets, a very apt and evocative image, while grasshoppers stand for the land-based forces. The plague released was devastating to the German powers who eventually capitulated and withdrew. France was liberated and the German armies surrendered in 1945.

The Separation of Charles and Diana

Ignorant envy being supported by the great King

Shall talk of prohibiting the writings,

His wife no wife, being tempted by another,

Shall no more than they two prevail by crying.

(Verse 57)

There are several references in the quatrains to the relationship between Prince Charles and Princess Diana and the rumours of their affairs. Those close to the 'great King' try to suppress information about his indiscretions, but the King's mistress persuades him to the contrary. In previous times, such information would have been kept close to the royal family, but in our modern age when every little move is under the scrutiny of the press hounds, it becomes almost impossible to keep such matters a secret. This would then influence a decision to try to be open, even about such private affairs including the will of Princess Diana.

The Downfall of President Nixon

The old man shall be baffled and deprived of his place,

By the stranger that shall have instigated him,

But his sons shall be eaten before his face,

The brother at Chartres, Orléans shall betray Rouen.

(Verse 61)

Here we have a quatrain related to the demise of President Richard Nixon whose 'sons', or Republican party colleagues, were soundly defeated after the Watergate scandal of 1972. The pressure on Nixon grew to be so great, following the revelation of the cover-up of malpractice within the Nixon administration, that his resignation in 1974 became inevitable. Nostradamus can be relied upon to throw new light on such high affairs of state, whether they be of his own time, of ours, or even beyond.

Left: Nostradamus referred to the troubled relationship of Prince Charles and Princess Diana, and to their ultimate separation.

Opposite top: The attack on the American fleet at Pearl Harbor in 1941.

Opposite below: Oil wells were still burning in Northern Kuwait almost one year after the Gulf War of 1991.

Fires in Kuwait after the Gulf War

In the year that Saturn and Mars shall be fiery,

The air shall be very dry, in many countries,

By secret fires, many places shall be burnt with heat,

There shall be scarcity of rain, hot winds, wars, wounds.

(Verse 67)

In their analysis of the human condition, both for medical and philosophical purposes, physicians such as Nostradamus placed great store on the balance within the body of the four humours, these being said to be either dry, moist, hot or cold. Nostradamus extended the notion of their combination and the resulting balance to national and political affairs. Here is a reference to an imbalance of fire and heat, resulting in the devastation and fires that afflicted Kuwait in the wake of the Gulf War of 1991 when oil wells were deliberately set ablaze by the occupying Iraqi forces.

Pearl Harbor

One being ready to fight shall faint,

The chief of the adverse party shall obtain the victory,

The rear guard shall fight it out,

Those that fall away shall die in the white country.

(Verse 75)

During the Second World War Japan at first misled the USA by attacking islands in the Pacific, but not the US naval base at Pearl Harbor. But then a surprise attack was made on the American fleet in December 1941. This was a political mistake by Japan as the action brought America firmly into the Second World War on the side of the Allies, when previously this country had avoided being drawn up into the conflict. American victories developed in the course of rearguard actions against Japanese resistance on many islands. This was all foreseen by Nostradamus.

Century V

Conflict in Northern Ireland

Before the coming of the ruin of the Celts,

Two shall discourse together in the church,

Dagger in the heart of one, on horseback and spurring,

Without noise they shall bury the great one.

(Verse 1)

Nostradamus accurately predicted the ongoing 'troubles' in Northern Ireland, foreseeing that ruin would come to many of the Irish Celtic race as a result of the conflict. This was originally a conflict between Protestant and Catholic on religious grounds but now the divide is chiefly a political one, even though the battle lines are still drawn up between Protestant and Catholic. The implication is that everyone loses, the 'great one' being the country of Ireland as a whole. A pointless struggle, pointless as far as the violence is concerned, that is. Political ends were never to be achieved in this way; it is dialogue that will win the day.

Naval Warfare

The fire shall be left burning, the dead shall be hid,

Within the globes terrible and fearful,

By night the fleet shall shoot against the city,

The city shall be on fire, the enemy shall be favourable to it.

(Verse 8)

Nostradamus predicts the use of terrible weapons launched from sea-borne vessels, equipped for warfare. Interpreters have suggested that this quatrain suggests nuclear warfare and the devastation it causes. More recent suggestions, with the benefit of hindsight, have linked this prediction with the fires in Kuwait, left burning when the Iraqi troops were forced to release their hold over Kuwait during the Gulf War of 1991 and retreat. Many oil wells were deliberately set on fire during this retreat.

Below: The Easter Rising in Ireland.

Napoleon's Army Crosses the Alps

Beyond the Alps shall a great army go,

And a little while before shall be born a wretched monster,

Prodigious and suddenly the great Tuscan

Shall return to his own nearest place.

(Verse 20)

This is a prediction that Napoleon would cross the Alps with a great army. Nostradamus also foretells the exile of Napoleon to the island of Elba and then his return to Corsica, to 'his own nearest place'.

Nostradamus's considerable concern for French political history is quite understandable given his own French nationality and roots. It is remarkable that his writings were so universal, with his predictions looking much further afield than his native country.

Above: Nostradamus made many predictions relating to Napoleon Bonaparte.

The Decadent Court of Louis XV

The Kingdom and King being joined under Venus,

Saturn shall have power over Jupiter,

The law and reign raised by the Sun,

Shall be put to the worse by the Saturnians.

(Verse 24)

Saturnine revels were the order of the day in the 18th century at the corrupt and frivolous court of Louis XV of France, the revels being led by Madame du Barry. It was a time when law and order were made a mockery. Such a state of affairs could never endure at a court which enjoyed such influence and power and eventually it became the source of its own undoing. Venus is the goddess of love, but she also rules excesses and lavish waste, gluttony and immorality. For a time nothing could be done about the injustices and excesses of the court's behaviour because they were performed in the name of the Sun, the King.

Dismantling of the USSR

The Slavic Nation shall by martial luck,

Be raised to so high a degree,

That they shall change their Prince and elect one

among themselves.

They shall cross the sea with an army raised in

the mountains.

(Verse 26)

Nostradamus foresaw the train of events that unfolded in the course of the 20th century when he described the development of the USSR through a revolution that first involved a change in the form of government, and the instigation of a Communist regime. This then grew to attain such power that many other countries came under its sway. Later though, the union was disbanded, resulting in further revolution in many of the Eastern Bloc countries.

Sexual Freedom and Immorality

By the pleasure of a voluptuous edict,

The poison shall be mixed with the law,

Venus shall be in so great request,

That it shall darken all the alloy of the Sun.

(Verse 72)

Nostradamus here uses the image of Venus, in her negative aspect the bringer of immorality, excess, waste and unlimited sexual freedoms. He sees that moral codes will be utterly inadequate and regards the onset of liberal ideas and ideals with unease. Nostradamus would not have felt at home in the Swinging Sixties or the Naughty Nineties. He regarded liberal ideas as 'poison'.

Recurrent Turmoil in the Greek State

A King shall be, who shall be of the opposite,

To the banished persons raised upon the Kingdom,

The chaste Hippolite nation shall swim in blood,

And shall flourish a great while under such a design.

(Verse 52)

From 1832 to 1967 Greece was ruled by four different kings with intermittent bloody strife intervening several times, culminating with the removal of King Constantine II by a military junta in 1967. In this context it is possible to see how Nostradamus was here predicting the recurrent turmoil affecting Greece and its government. This is a European country that has experienced so little stability that it has been unable to flourish as it should. Any individuals or governments who seemed to flourish during this period only did so for a very short time.

Right: Nostradamus foretold of the development of the USSR through a revolution that involved the formation of a Communist regime. He also predicted that the union would be dismantled, resulting in further revolution. Below: The establishment of liberal attitudes to sexual freedom and immorality were seen as poison by the morally-minded prophet.

The Occupation of Paris

Divided in two heads and parted in three arms,

The great city shall be troubled with waters,

Some great ones among them scattered by banishment,

By a Persian head, Turkey shall be much oppressed.

(Verse 86)

This is the occasion of the surrender of Paris to Nazi Germany on 14 June, 1940, the city subsequently being overrun by German troops. French leaders scattered for their own safety, and at the same time there was much unrest in the East (Russia) as Hitler attacked the Russians on 22 June, 1941. Europe was beleaguered and it seemed there would be no stopping the advance of the Nazi cause. Virtually every nation in Europe was at this time living in fear.

Rising Up of the Scottish Nation

Under the territory of the round lunary globe,

When Mercury shall be lord of the ascendant,

The Island of Scotland shall make a luminary,

That shall put the English to a revolution.

(Verse 93)

Of contemporary interest, this quatrain foretells the rising up of the Scottish nation. A great force or light will arise from this nation, bringing about a revolution in England. Perhaps the process has already started with the referendum in 1997 which overwhelmingly gave the UK government a mandate to set up a Scottish parliament. Time will tell whether this parliament becomes the great luminary that Nostradamus predicted.

Roosevelt's Rise to Power

In the middle of the great world shall be the rose,

For new deeds, blood shall be publicly spilt,

To say the truth, every one shall close his mouth,

Then at the time will be the one long looked for.

(Verse 96)

This prediction contains an example of the way Nostradamus sometimes would play on words. His clue towards the identity of a great world leader is contained in the two words 'rose' and 'world', which is 'Welt' in German. Rosewelt is the combination, and President Roosevelt is the world leader who emerges. There are many such examples scattered throughout the quatrains which make the interpretation particularly interesting. Rather like cracking a code, when you discover what Nostradamus means, the obscure becomes the obvious.

Left: Nostradamus predicts that the Scottish nation will rise up.
Above: American President Roosevelt became a world leader.
Opposite: The taking of the Louvre during the French Revolution.

Century VI

The Greenhouse Effect

So great a famine with a plague,

Through a long rain shall come along the Arctic Pole,

Samarobryn a hundred leagues from the hemisphere,

Shall live without law, exempt from politics.

(Verse 5)

There are two significant interpretations for this prediction and both could be closely connected. The suggestion is that the Northern Hemisphere will suffer from a devastating plague followed by a period of anarchy throughout the affected countries. It is also taken by some interpreters to predict the damage to the ozone layer that is occurring in the Earth's atmosphere and the resultant Greenhouse Effect which has potentially devastating results for the planet.

The French Revolution

Despite the King, the coin will be brought lower,

The people shall rise against their King,

Peace being made, holy laws made worse,

Paris was never in such a great disorder.

(Verse 23)

An interesting characteristic of this stanza is that the predictions it recounts pertaining to the French Revolution of 1789 are in their correct chronological order. First came the collapse of the country's financial structure which was followed by a general uprising and revolution. The results included the abandoning of religion and the unleashing of anarchic disorder in Paris. The effects of the French Revolution altered the whole course of the country's future.

The Order of St Francis

At the founding of a new sect,

The bones of the great Roman shall be found,

The Sepulchre shall appear covered with marble,

The earth shall quake in April, they shall be ill-buried.

(Verse 66)

Again this verse contains the essence of two predictions. It talks about the order formed by St Francis of Assisi, linking this prediction with the city of San Francisco. This will be the sight of a huge earthquake occurring in April, in similar fashion to the 'quake of April 1906. It is not really a question of whether such an earthquake will occur, but when, the city living in constant expectation of major tremors. Modern buildings and roads are much more secure and can withstand earth tremors better than their counterparts at the beginning of the century, but the risk of severe damage is still high.

Saddam Hussein's Rule

The great carpet folded shall not show,

But by half the greatest part of the history,

The exiles of the kingdom shall appear sharp afar off.

In warlike matters everyone shall believe.

(Verse 61)

There is a reference here to Saddam Hussein's move to a secret location during the Gulf War of 1991, from where he was able to conduct his operations. In general, Nostradamus is referring to an exiled leader and the true historical facts which concern him. The truth as to how this leader was able to maintain a powerful influence even in exile from his homeland is concealed. This may refer to Saddam Hussein's future actions. It is clear that his story has not yet run its full course, according to recent events.

Above left: Saddam Hussein, President of Iraq.

Above: The painting 'Ecstacy of Saint Francis' by Pomponio Amalteo.

Opposite top: The execution of Marie Antoinette, Queen of France, 1793.

The Rise and Dominance of Communism

To the great Empire quite another shall come,

Being distant from goodness and happiness,

Governed by one of base parentage,

The Kingdom shall fall, a great unhappiness.

(Verse 67)

Nostradamus predicts the rise of the power of Communism (in other quatrains Nostradamus gives fuller details about its later collapse), the result of this being the subjugation of various 'kingdoms' (democracies) which suffer great unhappiness. Western democracies are the target of the expansionist Communist regime, which, in the Eastern Bloc, became a huge political force, pitted against the Western alliance of the USA and NATO. Economic forces eventually caused the collapse of the USSR leaving many countries in a state of turmoil and affecting practically every nation of the world in one way or another.

The Death of Marie Antoinette

By a feigned fury of divine inspiration,

The wife of the great one shall be ravished,

Judges willing to condemn such a doctrine,

A victim shall be sacrificed to the ignorant people.

(Verse 72)

This is Nostradamus's prediction of the fate of that evocative figure, Marie Antoinette, Queen of France. She was the wife of Louis XVI, and was caught up as a figurehead in the French Revolution of 1789. She was the victim of the mob's insatiable blood lust, condemned by her judges to face the guillotine. This she duly did in 1793, as witnessed by the 'ignorant people' of Paris. Nostradamus found it difficult to hide his opinion on these matters, and in receiving such predictions through his magical arts he would have suffered great anguish himself. Imagine the ability to foresee world events but without the power to alter their course.

The Spanish Civil War

The Kingdom of Fez shall come to those of Europe,

Fire and sword shall destroy their city,

The great one of Asia, by land and sea with a great army,

So that blues, greens, crosses to death he shall drive.

(Verse 80)

On reading this prediction, a contemporary observer of Nostradamus commented that this was a very strange prediction if it proved to be true. Nostradamus was describing the Spanish Civil War of 1936-39. Uprisings began in Morocco, spreading then to Spain. He even indicates the aid that was given to the Republicans by Russia and to General Franco by Germany. It would have been natural for Nostradamus's contemporaries to seek to apply his predictions to their own time. If Nostradamus was looking so far into the future, it is hardly surprising that many of his predictions were thought to be 'strange'.

The Munich Agreement

The stinking and abominable defiling,

After the deed shall be successful,

The great one excused for not being favourable,

That Neptune might be persuaded to peace.

(Verse 90)

Neptune, the ruler of the waves, in the guise here of British Prime Minister Neville Chamberlain, is persuaded to peace. This is the outcome of the infamous Munich Agreement, which was signed in 1938 by several nations as an agreement to non-aggression by ceding the Sudetenland in Czechoslovakia to Nazi Germany. The agreement was believed, and Chamberlain returned home to England to wave the infamous piece of paper in front of his nation's people. The paper was worth less than the ink used to write it. Peace was not preserved. It was not long before Hitler's intentions were made quite clear to all of Europe.

The Bombing of Hiroshima

Ruin shall happen to the Vandals that will be terrible,

Their great city shall be tainted, a pestilent deed;

They shall plunder Sun and Moon, and violate

their temples,

And two rivers shall be red with running blood.

(Verse 98)

Nostradamus predicts the terrible bombing of Hiroshima with atomic weapons that happened in 1945. Hiroshima's location between two rivers is described together with its Japanese temples. Such events, which affect so many people in such a terrible way, have cosmic and spiritual effects which reverberate through the universe and perhaps penetrate the veil of time. Nostradamus was able to sense these reverberations as they were transmitted back through time to connect with his own subconscious mind.

Cataclysmic Fire

The heavens shall burn at five and forty degrees,

The fire shall come near the great new city,

In an instant a great flame dispersed shall burst out,

When they shall make a trial of the Normans.

(Verse 97)

Here's one that may worry a few people! The prediction is that a great fire will envelop and devastate the greatest and newest of the world's major cities. Nostradamus pinpoints these to be positioned close to the 45th parallel and a quick glance at the atlas shows the following cities to be threatened by this prognostication: New York, Chicago, Minneapolis, Bucharest, Belgrade, Rome, Paris and Madrid. A chastening thought.

Opposite: Franco's troops in battle during the Spanish Civil War, 1938.
Above: Nostradamus predicts cataclysmic fire in cities close to the 45th parallel.
Right: Nostradamus prophesied the atomic bombing of Hiroshima in 1945.

Century VII

The Use of Laser Beams

Arles shall not proceed by open war,

By night the soldiers shall be astonished,

Black, white, and blue dissembled on the ground,

Under the feigned shadow will be proclaimed traitors.

(Verse 2)

Commentators have pointed out that 'Arles' is an anagram for 'laser' which allows this quatrain to be interpreted in the context of laser technology being used in warfare. Lasers are particularly useful for guided weaponry, and are as effective in nighttime as they are during the day. Remember that at the time when he was writing, Nostradamus would have had no concept about the production of coherent light beams, and still less regarding the use to which they could be put.

The East-West Conflict

At the fight of the great light horsemen,

They shall cry out, confound the great crescent,

By night they shall kill sheep dressed as shepherds,

Red abysms shall be in the deep ditch.

(Verse 7)

Whereas a previous quatrain predicts the rise of Communism in the Eastern bloc countries, this verse predicts the collapse of the communist Soviet Union at the end of the 1980s. The verse is a description of East-West conflict, the 'great crescent' being a reference to the emblematic Soviet sickle. The final line is a conclusive description of the defeat of the 'Reds' and everything that they stand for. This heralds the beginning of a new phase of turmoil leading towards the major political and natural upheavals at the end of the millennium.

Charles De Gaulle

The great Prince dwelling near Le Mans,

Stout and valiant, general of a great army,

Of Britons and Normans by sea and land,

Ravaging Cape Barcelona and plunder the Island.

(Verse 10)

The French general referred to here is a charismatic figure who captures the hearts of his people, is strong and resolute. His bravery and military bearing are the result of great deeds at the head of a powerful army. Not only does this general command military power, but political power also. He rules by common consent not force, and is able to extend the range of his influence beyond the borders of France. Nostradamus provides a descriptive prediction of Charles De Gaulle, President of France from 1959 to 1969.

Louis XIII Wages War

The Royal Infant shall despise his mother,

Eye, feet wounded, rude, disobedient,

News to a lady very strange and bitter,

There shall be killed about five hundred.

(Verse 11)

At the age of fifteen years, in 1615, Louis XIII, King of France was persuaded to make war against his mother, Marie de Médici, who was then Regent of the Kingdom. As a result, a battle took place in which 500 of the Queen's soldiers were killed. This is one of the clearer predictions in that neither symbolism nor coded language are used to cover Nostradamus's tracks.

Opposite: General Charles De Gaulle, President of France from 1959 to 1969.

An Increase in Religious Sects

They shall show topography falsely,

The urns of the monuments shall be open,

Sects shall multiply and holy philosophy,

Shall give black for white and green for gold.

(Verse 14)

This is a prediction that indicates that a proliferation of religious sects will herald the break-up of the established church. The increase in popularity of sects is a result of lack of honesty in the church ('black for white') and in turn causes great arguments and conflict in the church. The establishment is shown to have described the nature of spirituality (its 'topography') falsely, and its innermost falsehood is lain bare for all to see. The old religion dies and people turn to new ones for succour and support.

Gambling in Monte Carlo

The Nicene fort shall not be fought against,

By shining metal it shall be overcome,

The doing of it shall a long time be debated,

It shall be a strange fearful thing to the citizens.

(Verse 19)

Nostradamus's predictions are quite moralistic in their tone, and not simply because he sees so much evil in the world brought about through violence and wars. He also identifies sex and gambling! This quatrain contains a reference to gold, the 'shining metal', that most coveted of precious metals. In this verse he predicts and condemns the activities at the Casino of Monte Carlo (Monaco), which is adjacent to Nice on the south coast of France, and has long been associated with the gaining or losing of fortunes at the fall of a dice.

The Abdication of the Iranian Shah

The Royal Sceptre shall be constrained to take

What his predecessors had mortgaged,

After that they shall misinform the lamb,

When they shall come to plunder the palace.

(Verse 23)

When the Shah of Iran was forced to abdicate in 1979, the assets of his Pahlavi dynasty were plundered and used to obtain military hardware, aeroplanes and sophisticated armaments. The royal palace was literally plundered by the new regime under Khomeini to increase its own power and wealth. Nostradamus shows great concern for the events taking place this century in the Middle East, as he identifies this part of the world as the melting pot which will come to the boil as we approach the millennium.

Flying Boats

Flying boats and galleys round about seven ships,

Shall be in the livery of deadly war,

The chief of Madrid shall receive blows of oars,

Two shall escape, and five carried to land.

(Verse 26)

It is possible that the first two lines foretell the multiple nuclear warheads of the Trident missile, which are fired from underwater by submarines. The reference to 'flying boats' could refer to the original Howard Hughes 'Spruce Goose' aircraft or the first Pan American Airways Clipper which landed on water. Nostradamus seems to have had a nose not only for catastrophe and disaster, but for scientific and technological advancement too, although he would surely be amazed to discover the modern reality of his predictions.

Opposite top: The Casino of Monte Carlo, Monaco.

Above: Nostradamus predicted flying boats that could land on water.

The Alliance between Hitler and Mussolini

By fraud a kingdom and army shall be despoiled,

The fleet shall be possessed, passages shall be made to spies,

Two feigned friends shall agree together,

They shall raise up a hatred that had long been dormant.

(Verse 33)

Nostradamus is here predicting a deadly alliance between two fascist dictators who knew how to make full use of the policy of divide and conquer. Their technique was based on the consistent and continuous use of propaganda which roused 'a hatred that had long been dormant', namely the fatal prejudices of anti-Semitism. Nostradamus would have been familiar both with the type of powerhungry individual that Hitler and Mussolini represented, and the violence of anti-Semitic hatred from which his own family suffered first-hand experience. This was surely a painful prophecy.

A Ghostly Haunting

The bones of the feet and hands in shackles,

By a noise a house shall be a long time deserted,

By a dream the buried shall be taken out of the ground,

The house shall be salubrious, and inhabited without noise.

(Verse 41)

There is no time nor place indicated here, but Nostradamus has a very strong vision of a ghostly haunting. The house he sees lying empty for a long time as the result of its habitation by restless spirits, energies with which he would have been personally familiar. These ghosts go their own way through the house 'without noise', the consequence of the desecration of a grave. Nostradamus was sensitive to this happening to his own grave as has been explained in the introduction to *The Centuries*. Perhaps Nostradamus knew exactly where the house to which he referred was situated, but preferred for personal reasons not to reveal its whereabouts.

Century VIII

Economic Plight

The great credit, of gold, of silver, great abundance,

Shall blind honour by lust,

The offence of the adulterer shall be known,

Which shall come to his great dishonour.

(Verse 14)

Nostradamus foresaw little positive news regarding the outlook for the 20th century. His vision for the latter part we will come to, but before this he foretold difficult problems for capitalist countries, for Communism and for the developing world – soaring inflation and currency devaluation, together with a universal laxity in morals with little social constraint. In particular the church's power wains with consequent lack of control over moral behaviour. In addition to this, he predicted the economic difficulties suffered by the church itself, with falling congregations in western countries, together with mismanagement of church assets.

Opposite left: Nostradamus predicted a deadly alliance between the two fascist dictators Hitler and Mussolini.
Opposite right: The apparition of a ghost.
Right: Pope John Paul II.

Perils For The Pope

To maintain the great troubled cloak,

The red ones shall march to clear it,

A family shall be almost crushed to death,

The red reds shall knock down the red one.

(Verse 19)

This verse is generally now taken to predict the assassination attempt on Pope John Paul II in 1983. It is interpreted as a dire warning for the papacy. The red ones are cardinals, the red reds terrorists. According to Nostradamus, the red reds kill a cardinal and cause subsequent death also to many others in a crowd panic. Nostradamus foretells elsewhere of the decline and indeed disintegration of the Christian churches, an event which is beginning to unfold at the end of the 20th century.

A Major Discovery

From Catons found in Barcelona,

Found discovered, in place of soil and ruin,

The great that hold, will not Pampelone,

By the abbey of Montserrat, a fine rain.

(Verse 26)

Not everything that Nostradamus predicts is of ruin and disaster. Occasionally a verse points to a new discovery that will have potential great benefit. Here he suggests perhaps that the discovery of a new plant could greatly benefit the poor people of Europe. It has properties such that it can be eaten, and it could even become a staple food. The clues are all there for intrepid detectives to search out the significance and meaning of this potential life-saver.

Below: Unusual weather is being experienced in many parts of the world.

Unusual Weather Patterns

Within the entrance of Garonne and Blaye,

And the forest not far from Damazan,

Of discoveries of frozen seas, then hail and north wind,

Dordonnois frozen by the error of Mezan.

(Verse 35)

It is not only wars and political upheaval that cause great difficulties for common folk, but the weather too. Nostradamus always had an eye for the climate and here he is predicting the results of the Greenhouse Effect. He describes a particularly bad winter in Europe when rivers freeze and violent winds and hailstorms ravage town and country alike. The change in the weather patterns of the late 20th century brings with it not only climatic change, but potential changes to the geography of some coastlines as some land disappears and other areas surface.

The Beheading of King Charles I

The fortress near the Thames,

Shall fall, then the King that was kept within

Shall be seen near the bridge in his shirt,

One dead before, then in the fort kept close.

(Verse 37)

After his defeat on 23 December, 1648, King Charles I was brought to Windsor Castle, overlooking the Thames. It is told how he was dressed in a white shirt as he was taken forth in January 1649 and beheaded before a crowd in London. This is a classic Nostradamus prediction, in that it is possible to see how explicit it is after the event, but before it, the verse would have seemed enigmatic in the extreme. The same applies to his predictions for the years to come, which still seem unclear in their detail but quite clear in the sense of their general outcome. The detail may soon become clear to us.

Left: King Charles I of England was executed in January 1649.

The Liberation of Kuwait

Saturn in Cancer, Jupiter with Mars,

In February Caldondon, ground saved,

The Republic assaulted on three sides,

Near Verbiesque, fight and mortal war.

(Verse 48)

Here we can see some of the astrological events which gave Nostradamus clues as to what his own psychic transmissions implied, and when they would come about. He makes repeated warning of a great war and prophesies the liberation of Kuwait from Iraqi invasion by the United States and her allies in February 1991. The meaning of Nostradamus's visions would have often remained unclear even to him until he was able to analyze them in the light of astrological events.

Famine in Africa

The plague shall be round about Capadillo,

Another famine cometh near to that of Sagunce,

The knight bastard of the good old man,

Shall cause the great one of Tunis to be beheaded.

(Verse 50)

This prediction describes how drought, famine and disease plague West Africa from 1975 on. The great one of Tunis is Habib Bourguiba, President of Tunisia. He was re-elected to his fourth five-year term in 1974, and then in 1975 was elected president for life. Bourguiba was deposed from power in a bloodless revolution in 1987. However, Nostradamus predicts his death by violent means.

Oliver Cromwell

From a simple soldier, he shall come to have supreme command,

From a short gown he shall come to long one,

Valiant in arms, no worse man in the church,

He shall vex the priests, as water does a sponge.

(Verse 57)

From being a simple soldier, Oliver Cromwell rose to become the Lord Protector of the Commonwealth (1653-58), taking a degree from Oxford on the way. From a student in the university (a short gown), he became a graduate (taking a long one). There can be no doubt that in his day no-one caused the clergy more vexation than Cromwell, the devout Puritan. This is a very accurate description of the man, illustrating that Nostradamus could paint portraits without even knowing who the sitter was – warts and all!

Above: Nostradamus predicted plague and famine in Africa.

Above right: Oliver Cromwell, Lord Protector of the Commonwealth.

The Role of Germany in the Two World Wars

Twice set up high, and twice brought down,

The East also the West shall weaken,

His adversary after many fights,

Expelled by sea, shall fail in need.

(Verse 59)

The impulse behind German aggression that led to both World Wars was the desire for domination over as much of the world as possible and the establishment of a German empire. Nostradamus in his verses presents an overall picture of conflict with Germany in the 20th century, giving a description of the political aims behind the aggression, the course of events and even predicting the fortunes of the main adversaries. In each of the two World Wars, Germany was defeated after untold suffering on all sides.

New Energy Sources

Through the abundance of the army scattered,

High will be low, low will be high,

Too great a faith, a life lost in jesting,

To die by thirst, through abundance of want.

(Verse 100)

Automation and the discovery of new sources of energy completely revolutionize the way the labour force and the economic landscape is organized. Such discoveries – yet to come – will remove one of the reasons for wars of aggression because the natural resources that create power and, therefore, wealth will be available to all. Nostradamus prophesies this as coming about in times to come, when the natural order is turned on its head, when 'low will be high'.

Below: German soldiers in battle during the Second World War.

Century IX

Opening Tutankhamen's Tomb

He that shall open the found sepulchre,

And shall not close it again promptly,

Evil will befall him and he shall not be able to prove

Whether is best, a British or Norman King.

(Verse 7)

Nostradamus prophesied – or perhaps even created – the notion that if his own tomb were opened for any length of time, then evil would befall the person or people who committed the act (see pages 24-25). Here he applies this thought to an even more famous tomb, that of the Egyptian boy-king Tutankhamen (d.c. 1340BC). The opening of the tomb in 1922 brought sudden and mysterious death to its discoverer, Lord Carnarvon, and to members of his family and entourage. There is a protective mystique which surrounds the dead. None more so than in this case.

Franco and the Spanish Civil War

From Spanish Franco shall come the assembly,

The Ambassador not pleased, shall make a separation,

Those of the Riviera, shall be in the mêlée,

And shall deny entry into the great gulf.

(Verse 16)

The reference here is to the Spanish Civil War and its repercussions, with the chief protagonist explicitly named as 'Franco'. Nostradamus was inconsistent in his ability to name names exactly, but here he does so with great accuracy. The quatrain is also interpreted as referring to the Axis powers of the Second World War who, after consultation with General Franco, were denied domination of Gibraltar and thus entrance to the 'great gulf' of the Mediterranean.

The Discovery of the Rosetta Stone

A deep column of fine Porphyry shall be found,

Under whose base shall be important writings,

Bones, hairs twisted, Roman force tried,

A fleet about the port of Methelin.

(Verse 32)

The importance of the Rosetta Stone lies in the fact that, because it had inscribed on it the same text in three languages, it provided a key to cracking the code of Egyptian hieroglyphics, thus opening up to us a previously hidden world of Egyptian life. The stone was discovered in 1799 near Rosetta in Egypt, and its inscription describes events that took place in 197-6 BC. The stone was probably buried by Roman legions in the early Christian era.

Opposite left: A gold mask from the tomb of the boy-king Tutankhamen.
Opposite right: General Franco. Below: The power of an atomic bomb.

The Advent of Atomic Power

Leave, leave, go forth out of Geneva all,

Saturn of gold shall be changed into iron,

The contrary of the positive ray shall exterminate all,

Before it happens, the Heavens shall show signs.

(Verse 44)

Nostradamus pulls no punches here in describing the ultimate devastation that nuclear power can bring about. The energy can be used positively but its opposite use is mightily destructive, capable of exterminating all. It is a clear warning of the results of mishandling this natural destructive force. There is a ray of hope, however, in that a clear sign will be given to show exactly what will happen before it comes about. Seeing the results of nuclear destruction in a vision must have been a terrible experience for Nostradamus, even for a man used to dealing with death and trying to prevent it through his healing work.

The Downfall of the Nazi Regime

He shall never be weary of asking,

Great Liar shall obtain his dominion,

Far from the court he shall be countermanded,

Piedmont, Picardy, Paris, Tyrhenia the worse.

(Verse 45)

Islamic Revolution

The undersigned to a worthless deliverance,

Shall have from the multitude a contrary advice,

Changing their monarch and put him in peril,

They shall see themselves shut up in a cage.

(Verse 47)

This indicates the final downfall of the Nazi regime, and emphasizes the doctrine of lies and deceit upon which it was built. Disturbingly, Nostradamus foresees the advent of the White Supremacist Movement and the continuation of fascism. The Supremacists hold the deluded belief that the Holocaust did not really happen, a remarkable case of closing ones eyes to reality.

Above: Islamic revolutionary soldiers in Iran.

A sign of our times is predicted here with the Islamic revolution in Iran. In many Islamic countries there has been a lurch towards religious fundamentalism, partly as a reaction to liberal ideas and what is perceived to be decadence and the influence of imperialism. Nostradamus also tells us that the leaders of this revolution become isolated within their own countries, creating extreme forms of nationalism. Does this herald another great uprising and invasion of Europe by Islamic forces?

Prediction of Great Hurricanes

The great maritime city of the ocean,

Encompassed with marshes of crystal,

In the winter solstice and the spring,

Shall be tempted with a fearful wind.

(Verse 48)

In particular, this predicts the occurrence of Hurricane Andrew off the coast of Florida in 1992. Still to come is the implication that a storm of similar destructive power will hit the city of London. Its people are warned of this hurricane which will cause considerable damage to the city. With our weather patterns now quite disturbed by the onset of global warming, it no longer seems unlikely that such an event may come to pass.

The Moon Landing

He shall come into the corner of Luna,

Where he shall be taken and put in a strange land,

The green fruits shall be in great disorder,

A great shame, to one shall be great praise.

(Verse 65)

The first two lines clearly predict the arrival of man on the Moon. This occurred in July 1969, when Apollo 11 landed in the Sea of Tranquillity and Neil Armstrong took the first 'small step for man'. This prediction is somewhat disconnected from the rest of the stanza, but this is not unusual for Nostradamus in that he often mixed up his predictions in different verses so that each might contain more than one particular reference.

Above: Nostradamus made an accurate prediction that mam would land on the surface of the Moon.

A New World Order

Once more shall the Holy Temple be polluted,

And depredated by the Senate of Toulouse,

Saturn two, three cycles revolving,

In April, May, people of a new leaven.

(Verse 72)

The First Night of the Gulf War

In a sea-fight night shall be overcome,

By fire, to the ship of the west, ruin shall happen,

A new stratagem, the great ship coloured,

Anger to the vanquished, and victory in a fog.

(Verse 100)

We now head into the realm of times to come in the next millennium with a startling prophecy that the world's religions will be completely revised in terms of their basic concepts and philosophy around the year 2150. Nostradamus suggests the rise of a new world order, perhaps with a unified religion which comes into being after a period of religious collapse. This is followed by an increase in the popularity of and a proliferation of religious sects. The new religion will rise like a phoenix out of the ashes of the old.

Nostradamus prophesies the first night of the Gulf War in January 1991. He sees in his vision a night battle involving naval vessels. He also sees that the bombardments are so ferocious that the night sky is illuminated so that it seems as light as day. His prediction tells of the demise of a particular vessel 'of the west' and also of the fog of war, the great confusion that arises as soon as hostilities begin.

Above: American troops prepare for battle during the Gulf War.

Century X

Defeat of the Spanish Armada

The galley and the ship shall hide their sails,

The great fleet shall make the little ones come out,

Ten ships approaching shall turn and push it,

The great being vanquished, they shall unite together.

(Verse 2)

When Nostradamus makes predictions about events which lie close to his own time, they become much clearer, as this one illustrates. The reason for this is that when he is prophesying events that for him will occur in the dim, distant future, he is dealing with images, ideas, and concepts that have no meaning for him in his own age. For example, the idea of laser beams or the concept of global warming are to us quite understandable realities, but for Nostradamus they would present him with images as apparently mythical as a unicorn. In the above quatrain, Nostradamus quite clearly sees the circumstances or the defeat of the Spanish Armada by the English fleet in August 1588, a mere 22 years after his death.

Conflict in the Falklands

Under the pasture of cud-chewing animals,

Conducted by them to the Herbipolique belly

Soldiers hidden, the weapons making a noise,

Shall be attempted not far from the Free City.

(Verse 13)

This is a prophecy of a scene much closer to our own times and is interpreted as representing the Falklands War when the United Kingdom regained the islands after an invasion by Argentinian armed forces in 1982. The 'shepherds' of the Falkland Islands, which is precisely how the UK government sees its role here, counterattack against the insurgent Argentinians. The prediction takes place not far from the 'Free City' of Port Stanley.

Below: There is little confusion surrounding Nostradamus's prediction that the Spanish Armada was to be defeated by the English fleet in 1588.

The Abdication of Edward VIII

Two quatrains are of interest here:

For not consenting to the divorce,

Which afterwards shall be acknowledged unworthy,

The King of the Island shall be expelled by force,

And another subrogated, who shall have no mark of

the King.

(Verse 22)

The circumstances of the abdication of King Edward VIII surrounded his commitment to an American commoner, Wallis Warfield Simpson, 'Mrs Simpson', whom he wished to marry but who was a divorcee. Pressure grew so great upon the King, both from his government and from the turmoil in his own heart, that he decided that his life was to be with the woman he loved, rather than as monarch of his country. The abdication took place in 1936.

The second quatrain enlarges on the subject and hints at the gossip which was directed at the conduct of Edward VIII and his future wife:

The young man born to the Kingdom of Britain,

Whom his father dying shall have recommended,

After his death, London shall give him a topic,

And shall ask the Kingdom away from his son.

(Verse 40)

Left: King Edward VIII abdicated the throne of Britain in 1936 to marry the American divorcee Wallis Simpson.
Right: Nostradamus pictured volcanic eruptions as he meditated in his study at night, and predicted widespread destruction surrounding Reggio in Italy.

Britain and America — a Special Relationship

The chief of London by rule of America,

The Island of Scotland shall be tempered by frost,

Kings and Priests shall have one who is a false

Anti-Christ,

Who will put them altogether in discord.

(Verse 66)

Perhaps this verse predicts the future when British and American leaders unite in a political venture setting up a dictator in a third country, who will in the end betray both his people and his political masters. This scenario is not so far-fetched considering the involvement of both countries in power-broking and gaining influence in countries possessing vital resources but not the capital to exploit them. Countries in the north of South America are prime candidates, and there is no doubt that this prospect has also been considered as far as the Iraqi leader Saddam Hussein is concerned.

Volcanic Eruptions

The eye of the object shall make such an excrescence,

Because so much, and so burning shall fall the snow,

The field watered shall come to decay,

That the primate shall succumb at Reggio.

(Verse 70)

The images in Nostradamus's mind's eye when he meditated in his study at night must often have had the quality of volcanic eruptions as they exploded into his consciousness. Here he predicts an actual volcanic eruption at Reggio in Italy. The eruption causes widespread destruction spraying out hot embers which fall like snow, destroying crops and vegetation in the surrounding countryside. Interpreters must decide whether the eruption is actually a physical one, or if this is symbolic of some other type of disturbance?

World Revolution

In the year 1999 and seven months,

From the skies shall come an alarmingly powerful king,

To raise again the great King of the Jacquerie,

Before and after, Mars shall reign at will.

(Verse 72)

Here Nostradamus reveals a prediction that must concern us for the future. He predicts a tremendous world upheaval in 1999. In this short verse, Nostradamus's interpreters have seen solutions to the great secret of the Book of Revelations regarding the final apocalypse that it envisions. Is this to be a 'War of the Worlds'? King of Jacquerie in the French verse is *Roy d'Angolmois*, an anagram for Roi de Mongolois – King of the Mongolians. Will the great threat come from the east – China or Mongolia?

Communications Technology

The old roads shall be made more beautiful,

There shall be a passage to Memphis summarily,

The great Mercury of Hercules, fleur-de-lys,

Making the earth, the sea and the countries to quake.

(Verse 79)

The Birth of Prince William

The natural to one so high, high not low,

The late return shall make the sad contented.

The Reconciled shall not be without strife,

In employing and losing all the time.

(Verse 84)

Nostradamus talks about the time of increased and varied means of communication between the countries of the world. Again he has the vision but not the available concepts to put his predictions about modern technology into words. This is as close as he can get to talking about such developments as the Internet and World Wide Web, fibre-optic communication, the information superhighway and satellite communication, all of these things coming under the astrological rulership of Mercury.

The message behind the interpretation of this quatrain, which predicts the birth of Prince William, Princess Diana's first child, in 1982, is that his demeanour and character would win approval from all sides, including the most staunch anti-royalist factions. Nostradamus was a royalist in his own sympathies and would have taken delight in witnessing such an event in our age.

Above: Princess Diana posed with her first child, Prince William.

A United States of Europe

As a Griffon shall come the King of Europe,

Accompanied by those of the North,

Of reds and whites shall conduct a great troop,

And then, shall go against the King of Babylon.

(Verse 86)

Nostradamus foretells a United States of Europe under the leadership of Russia, opposing the forces of Mammon. The Griffon, a mythical monster, half lion and half eagle, was supposed to keep watch of the gold of Russia. This prediction seems unlikely from our current point of view, particularly in the light of Russia's decline in power since the end of the Cold War. However, it is possible to envisage events that could lead to such a state of affairs and once a political move is set in motion, events can happen quickly.

A Golden Age

The walls shall be turned from brick into marble,

There shall be peace for seven and fifty years,

Joy to mankind; the aqueduct shall be rebuilt,

Health, abundance of fruits, joys and a mellifluous time.

(Verse 89)

This optimistic verse brings this section to a close. In the next section we will examine Nostradamus's prophecies for our future. Many of these have a flavour of the apocalypse about them, so perhaps it is right to conclude here on a positive note. Nostradamus predicts a golden age of peace and happiness for mankind following a great war amongst nations. Let us hope that we all survive to experience such an age and can then ensure that it continues for as long as possible in the 21st century.

Modern Times and the Millennium

aving studied all the evidence that Nostradamus puts before us, how are we to judge him? If it is true that his prophecies are accurate, and we have the evidence now to examine this assertion with regard to the years that have passed since his death and now, how should we view his predictions for the years that are still to come? We can examine now what Nostradamus has to say about our futures.

Laws of Prophecy

Peter Lemesurier in a recent book, *Nostradamus, The Next Fifty Years*, suggests some 'laws' which will help us to sift through the evidence that Nostradamus provides for us. These are as follows: the most likely outcome is the one that nobody anticipates. The most obvious interpretation is likely to be the wrong one. Preconception and prophecy do not mix. Prophecies tend to be self-fulfilling. A prophecy's accuracy decreases as the square of the time to its fulfilment. Prophecy and interpretation are incompatible activities. Clairvoyance foreshortens the future. If it can happen, it will; if it can't happen, it might.

Basically, these rules suggest that great care has to be taken when interpreting Nostradamus. They persuade us that the process is not straightforward, but that if we observe these rules then we are much more likely to end up with a valid prediction.

Also, it is necessary to take fallibility into account. Nostradamus would have been the last person to suggest that every one of his prophecies would prove to be accurate, and he even admits as such. Also, Nostradamus possessed strong religious, biblical opinions which must also be taken into account when interpreting his predictions. For example, his view of the coming of an Antichrist must be

tempered by the knowledge that he would have used the term much more loosely than we might do now, perhaps regarding anyone who displayed immoral tendencies as a candidate for this title.

In this light, dictators such as Napoleon, Stalin and Hitler may already have fulfilled Nostradamus's prophecy regarding the coming of an Antichrist. Similarly, his views about the end of the world are highly coloured by biblical conceptions of the Apocalypse.

Nostradamus needs to be interpreted in a particular context. And we have already seen how his verses need hard work even to begin to decode them. Having said all this, an admission of the negative downside of our work, when all the difficulties have been surmounted, what is the end result? The following are quotations from authors who have spent considerable time and energy researching objectively into the prophecies of Nostradamus.

First of all a quotation from Nostradamus himself to his son and translator on 1 March, 1555:

> ...and I do not want to talk here of the years which have not yet transpired, but of your months of struggle during which you will not be capable in your deficient understanding of comprehending what I shall be constrained, after my death, to leave you.

Nostradamus is saying here that he knows what hard work it will be for his interpreters to make accurate sense of his predictions.

Opposite and above: It is possible that either the dictator Adolf Hitler or Napoleon Bonaparte may have fulfilled Nostradamus's prediction relating to the coming of an Antichrist.

Nostradamus's opponents are mostly people who do not really know the work but contest it because the little they do know of it upsets their personal convictions or beliefs. There are other sceptics (and they are more excusable), who have read translations that are as inaccurate as the original text… is accurate. When I recall my work in supplying half the text, with all the imperfections of which I am aware, I wonder how so many people can allow themselves to discuss, criticize and challenge the prophecy of Nostradamus. The widespread twentieth-century tendency in the West, where whatever one does is criticized and disputed even before its value is assessed, acts as a curb on the creative spirit.

Below: Albrecht Dürer's 'Apocalypse' is an allegorical representation of the Four Horsemen of the Apocalypse: War, Hunger, Plague and Death.

This is Jean-Charles de Fontbrune writing at the conclusion of his interesting and informative book *Nostradamus 1: Countdown To Apocalypse* (Pan Books), in which he suggests that critics of Nostradamus's writing are usually poorly qualified for their role.

Whether Nostradamus's predictions will turn out accurately to have reflected those forthcoming events is a moot point. But it is difficult to deny that, while his verses often do have a distinct air of déjà vu *about them, they also contain a large element that has no relevance to past events at all. They speak of air travel. They have the Asiatic invaders of Europe also moving into Persia, as well as overrunning Italy and France. They hint at the use of particularly nasty aerial weapons. They all but name Polaris and Trident. They spell out in enormous detail the various stages of a campaign in Western Europe that has no historical counterpart. They even set out some sort of time scale for the conflict which seems to have no relevance to history.*

In all these respects, then, those of Nostradamus's prophecies that clearly do not refer to the past still remain unfulfilled. At the same time they are remarkably detailed and consistent, constantly tying in one with the other. As a result they must for the most part either stand or fall together. All in all, then, these facts have to mean one of two things. Either the still-outstanding prophecies of Nostradamus are likely to be fulfilled in the future, more or less en bloc, or they are just plain wrong for page after page after page.

Peter Lemesurier in his original and provocative book *Nostradamus, The Next Fifty Years* (Piatkus Books), opines that it is either to be all or nothing as far as the future is concerned. While we can see in retrospect how Nostradamus's predictions as they related to our past may be at fault in their detail – or at fault in the way that they have been interpreted – for those predictions still to come, this is a different matter. Because his verses are so intertwined, because their content seems to be consistently interdependent, their relevance to the future will either be completely right or the opposite.

But for all the scholarly input, for all the psychological insights, for all the anagrams and puzzles solved, there remains one enormous difficulty in the interpretation of Nostradamus. Every interpreter… approaches the quatrains weighed down by his or her own prejudices.

This is particularly obvious when we discuss Nostradamus's vision of the end of the world. In modern times, it has become almost orthodox doctrine among Nostradamus interpreters that the prophet foresaw nuclear Armageddon obliterating the human race around the year 2000.

It is with some relief that I can report, quite categorically, he did not. Although several of his prophecies for modern times are almost as disturbing.

This is J.H. Brennan writing in the introduction to his excellent book, *Nostradamus, Visions Of The Future* (Thorsons), in which he contradicts the accepted apocalyptic prophecies of gloom and doom. Before the casual observer has even begun to study Nostradamus, it is common to believe that he predicts that the end of our world will occur in a few years time. However, those who have studied him closely say that this is not so.

Above: This 16th century fresco represents the Ladder of Virtue and also shows the Last Judgement. These biblical themes were very familiar to the God-fearing Nostradamus.

View of a Modern Prophet

The introduction referred to the modern prophet, Edgar Cayce, and his view that many cataclysmic events would happen in the last 40 years or so of this century, particularly during the years approaching the millennium. He prophesied that the Earth will be broken up in the western portion of North America; the greater part of Japan will disappear into the sea; the upper portion of Europe will be changed in the twinkling of an eye; land will appear off the east coast of America; open waters will appear in Greenland; upheavals in the Arctic and in the Antarctic will make volcanoes erupt in the torrid areas; land will appear between Tierra del Fuego and Antarctica. He even suggested that a shifting of the poles will encourage warmer climates.

Modern prophets of doom abound and will surely increase during the period up until the millennium. Our Age of Uncertainty breeds fear and people are all too ready to believe prophecies of disaster. Certainly our world for many is an unhappy place to live in, and Armaggedon – for someone, somewhere – is always happening right now. Many people feel as if they are constantly living on the brink of disaster and if this is the case in their personal lives, the tendency is to project this gloomy vision onto the wider world which then appears itself to be poised on the brink.

Right: Modern prophets are still predicting doom and destruction, particularly as this millennium draws to an end, and a new one starts.

Into the Future

When a fish pond that was a meadow shall

be mowed,

Sagittarius being in the ascendant,

Plague, Famine, Death from the

military hand,

The Century approaches renewal.

(Century I, Verse 16)

Taken in the context of what has just been discussed, the final line of this stanza is particularly interesting, as Nostradamus speaks of 'renewal' as the century nears its close, suggesting better times ahead. This ties in with the ancient esoteric tradition of a dawning new age of Aquarius in which spiritual values would gradually take over from the prevailing materialism. Depressing though the news may seem at times, our age must be viewed from the perspective of a dramatically increased awareness of ecological issues, spiritual values and even concern about human rights. Change is occurring on a far wider scale than ever before in human history.

In the year 1999 and seven months,

From the skies shall come an alarmingly

powerful king,

To raise again the great King of the

Jacquerie,

Before and after, Mars shall reign at

will.

(Century X, Verse 72)

I have already briefly considered this quatrain in the previous chapter, but because of its relevance to the coming years, it is worth considering it further. It is certainly an

apocalyptic vision. Almost without exception, commentators have regarded it as predicting the end of the world, although there is nothing in the verse to indicate this is what Nostradamus really meant.

A film of some years ago on Nostradamus, starring Orson Welles, portrayed the 'alarmingly powerful king' as a devilishly handsome Arab in a blue turban. It is possible, however, that we are here again faced with the hypothesis of extra-terrestrial incursions. The result may be that warring factions bury their differences in the face of a common threat. Certainly any mention of Mars suggests military action.

It seems quite clear, however, that this stanza does not predict the end of the world, backed up by the evidence of Nostradamus's own predictions which cover the period of many years to come. Whatever occurs, it seems more and more likely that as time progresses and the space programme expands, that we shall have contact with life forms from another planet. Nostradamus seems quite clear about this possibility and alludes to it in several of his predictions.

Above: It seems likely that Nostradamus believed that the Earth would be visited by powerful extra-terrestrial forces. Accounts of UFO visitations and alien abduction abound in the modern world.

The End of the World

Twenty years of the reign of the Moon
have passed,
Seven thousand years another shall hold his
monarchy,
When the Sun shall resume his days past,
Then is fulfilled and ends my prophecy.

(Century I, Verse 48)

Below: Nostradamus prophesies that the end of the world will occur in the year 7000, when the Sun will destroy the Earth.

Nostradamus explicitly prophesies the end of the world. In the year 7000 the Sun will destroy the Earth and again resume its undisputed way. Perhaps some huge solar eruption will engulf the Earth. A study of Nostradamus's predictions reveal that he has much to say about events that will occur far beyond the supposed cataclysmic times of the approaching millennium years. One verse, for example, (Century X, Verse 67) firmly places the end of the world in the year AD 3797, with a 'very mighty 'quake in the month of May'.

Certainly we are in for a continuing period of dramatic change, politically, technologically and in terms of the environment. 'The end of the world' should, I believe, be understood not in relation to one particular moment in time, but to many moments in time, as the old world dies to be born anew.

Renewal should be the keynote for Nostradamus's millennium and not death and decay. The world may not be the same tomorrow and in this way it will 'die'.

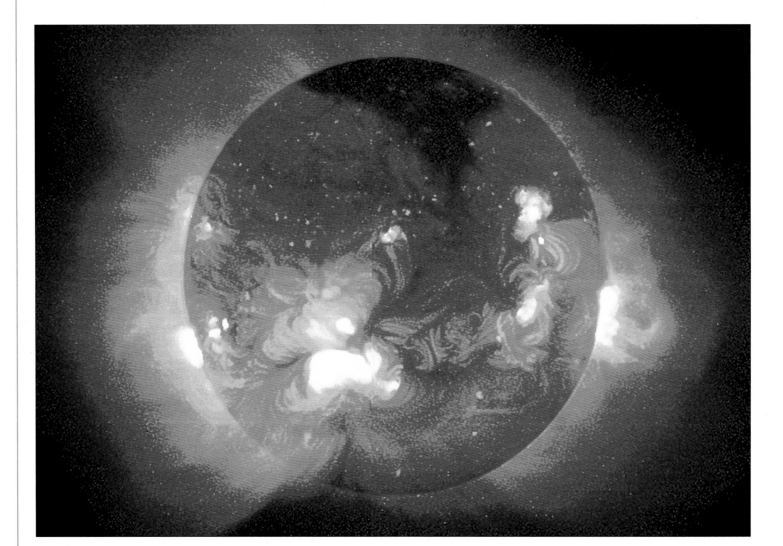

Who Would Be a Prophet?

The life of Nostradamus is not one to be envied. His was a life which experienced more than its fair share of suffering. But what he gave to us, he would have deemed worth the pain. He was a learned and sensitive man who did much to alleviate the suffering of others through his healing arts. He was a pioneer in the practice of medicine, but much more than this, he was a pioneer in the unexplored territory of the human mind.

He has left us markers on a journey which he took and which many others can now take, following in his footsteps, progressing further, perhaps redrawing his maps in a more accurate form. For the human mind is still the greatest unexplored territory of all. Despite the advancement of science and knowledge, the mystery of human consciousness is perhaps the greatest mystery of all still to be penetrated. I predict that the next millennium will bring about a greater understanding and charting of this relatively unknown territory; it seems clear that Nostradamus's contribution will be valued for ever more.

The most interesting thing is not even what Nostradamus predicted, nor whether his predictions prove to be accurate or not. What is amazing is that the human mind contains possibilities that are only limited by our imagination. Simply bring this idea into play and you are moving into the realm of Nostradamian magic. Transport yourself in your imagination to that little study room where Nostradamus conducted his prophetic experiments; see him at work and you will know what I mean.

As long as we are alive to the fact that many of Nostradamus's greatest predictions have actually come about, belong now to the past, and that history, particularly in terms of its darker moments, tends to repeat itself, then we are in a position to consider those predictions which have not yet been fulfilled.

Remember, finally, that Nostradamus's view of the future was essentially a modern one in that he believed in the possibility of multiple futures, futures whose realization lies in our hands today. He would have wanted us to build for the future, and most certainly not sit back and wait cynically for its destruction.

Below: Prophets are not generally accepted in their own time, and Nostradamus suffered for his unusual gifts. In his life he experienced much suffering and persecution as a result of his prophetic visions and texts.

Bibliography

There are literally hundreds of publications and books that have been published about Nostradamus. Of those still in print, the following are particularly useful and accessible:

The Complete Prophecies of Nostradamus
Translated, edited and interpreted by Henry C. Roberts, updated by Robert Lawrence, Thorsons.

This is a definitive collection of translated verses, the translations being used as the basis for this current book. They are freer from author bias than many other versions.

Nostradamus 1: Countdown to Apocalypse
Jean-Charles de Fontbrune, Pan Books. Also *Nostradamus 2: Into the Twenty-First Century* also published by Pan.

Well-researched and collated. This is a genuine and highly worthy appraisal of Nostradamus's work.

Nostradamus, The New Revelations
John Hogue, Element Books.

This is a highly illustrated book, packed with information and insight.

Nostradamus, The Next Fifty Years
Peter Lemesurier, Piatkus Books.

Not only has this book been well-researched and collated, but a lot of original and provocative thought is contributed by the author.

Nostradamus, Visions of the Future
J.H. Brennan, Thorsons.

An excellent introduction to Nostradamus, putting his prophecies into a detailed historical context, particularly the history of the 20th century.

Right: Capricorn, one of the signs of the Zodiac.
Opposite: A striking painting by Fra Angelico representing the Last Judgement and the torments of Hell.

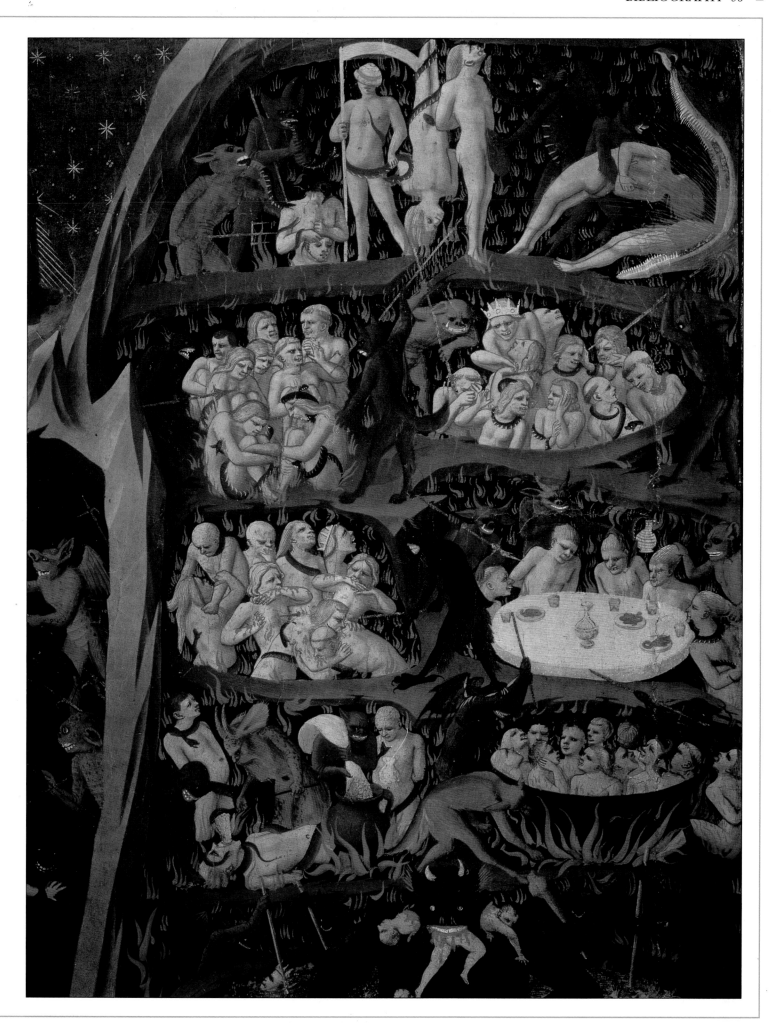

Your Prediction Notes

Index